PENGUIN BOOKS

Bollocks to Alton Towers

Bollocks to Alton Towers

Uncommonly British Days Out

ROBIN HALSTEAD

JASON HAZELEY

ALEX MORRIS

JOEL MORRIS

PENGUIN BOOKS

PENGUIN BOOKS

Published by the Penguin Group
Penguin Books Ltd, 80 Strand, London WC2R 0RL, England
Penguin Group (USA) Inc., 375 Hudson Street, New York, New York 10014, USA
Penguin Group (Canada), 90 Eglinton Avenue East, Suite 700, Toronto, Ontario, Canada M4P 2Y3
(a division of Pearson Penguin Canada Inc.)
Penguin Ireland, 25 St Stephen's Green, Dublin 2, Ireland (a division of Penguin Books Ltd)
Penguin Group (Australia), 250 Camberwell Road, Camberwell, Victoria 3124, Australia
(a division of Pearson Australia Group Pty Ltd)
Penguin Books India Pvt Ltd, 11 Community Centre,
Panchsheel Park, New Delhi – 110 017, India
Penguin Group (NZ), cnr Airborne and Rosedale Roads, Albany,
Auckland 1310, New Zealand (a division of Pearson New Zealand Ltd)
Penguin Books (South Africa) (Pty) Ltd, 24 Sturdee Avenue,
Rosebank, Johannesburg 2196, South Africa

Penguin Books Ltd, Registered Offices: 80 Strand, London WC2R 0RL, England

www.penguin.com

First published by Michael Joseph 2005
Published in Penguin Books 2006
11

Copyright © Robin Halstead, Jason Hazeley, Alex Morris and Joel Morris, 2005

The moral right of the authors has been asserted

All photographs are the property of the authors, except Exhibition Road (page 13 of Inset),
and Dennis Severs' House (page 18 of Inset)

Typeset by Rowland Phototypesetting Ltd, Bury St Edmunds, Suffolk
Printed in England by Clays Ltd, St Ives plc

ISBN-13: 978–0–141–02120–1
ISBN-10: 0–141–02120–9

www.bollockstoaltontowers.co.uk
www.framleyexaminer.com

For our parents

Contents

Contents

Introduction

If it is true that the British are a nation of animal lovers, then our favourite animal is probably the underdog.*

A Briton watching a sporting event in which he or she has no deep-seated preference for either team will naturally support the losing side until they pull in front, then swap allegiance. We watch the Eurovision Song Contest just to cheer on whichever nation is collecting the most Nul Points. We rightly applaud as one of our countrymen raises an Academy Award for the cameras of the press, then wait a couple of days and start carping about how the little upstart has got too big for his boots. It's because, deep down, we admire pluck far more than victory.

This book is a collection of the underdogs of

---

*In America, the home of bigness, betterness and the worship of the successful, the favourite animal is, conversely, the Top Cat.

British tourism. That doesn't mean they're not any good, quite the opposite in fact, but these are places that shun expensive showmanship and voguish technology in favour of something smaller, rarer and ultimately more satisfying. They require a little more effort and imagination (on occasion there's nothing to see at all) but they say more about Britain and the British than any number of corkscrew thrill rides or high-tech Interactive Visitor Experiences. The places we're recommending are small pleasures, but we, as a nation, do small better than almost anyone else.

The idea for this book, as is only right and proper, came while drunk. We were with friends, sharing some small-scale travellers' tales about a driving tour of regional museums we had made to research our last book (a parody of local history guides that sold nearly as many copies worldwide as a real local history guide). Soon the table was excitedly swapping stories of favourite unsung tourist backwaters. Everybody was passionate about at least one – some seemingly unprepossessing place full of unexpected delights, kept alive by the dedication of its staff, and founded on a belief that there might be just enough people interested in the development of butter churns in Dawlish Warren to keep the turnstiles clicking.

Over the next few months, we assembled a list of recommendations from anywhere and anyone we could. Slowly, a lovely image of a parallel Britain emerged: a Britain unconquered by branded megadrome franchises and pale imitations of successful international leisure formats. A stubbornly old-fashioned go-your-own-way Britain, where a day out could still involve a sensible family car, a tartan blanket, a Thermos of tea and three types of sandwich, two with chunky brown pickle. A Britain where filling your days off required a little bit of map-reading (furrowed brow, hard-sucked pipe) to discover a forgotten little corner unmarked by a queue of other visitors in hot cars.

We live in an increasingly patronising culture, where, to avoid alienating, frightening or confusing anyone who might otherwise spend some money, all the spiky edges have been smoothed off our fun.

Go to a theme park and get the same experience that's on offer in these parks from Frankfurt to Miami: a day out requiring nothing more specific from the visitor than an ability to feel queasy at speed. Go to a modern museum and be treated like a stroppy teenager, the whole institution seemingly terrified you'll start sulking that it's all 'Boooooooring' and stomp out because it's not a fairground. To avoid the possibility of your attention wandering for a moment, modern tourist attractions shepherd us, corral us, and titillate us simplistically. They make decisions for us as to what to see, where to go, how to have fun, all in the name of keeping us safely entertained. Nobody trusts us to play nicely on our own.

We decided to visit some tourist attractions that bucked that trend. In the noble tradition of the British amateur who builds a rocket in his shed without blueprints, we did absolutely no focus-grouping or market research. We simply made a list of the ones that sounded good and got on with it, relying on nothing more well thought through than an inarticulate leap of the heart at the sound of the place.

As we trotted round the country over the next nine months,* this random assortment of attractions

---

*Many of the attractions were visited by public transport. Since Britain is a nation of trainspotters, we felt it was right that we spend a lot of time peering at railway timetables in the rain and eating Travellers (sic) Fare sandwiches.

started to fall into some sort of shape. From what had initially been no more than a gut reaction that, yes, these were all Uncommonly British Days Out, a theme emerged. Eventually, we realised what all these places had in common: a characteristically British mistrust of ostentation, a love of the modest, the enthusiastic and the unusual. Sometimes they were defined as much by what they weren't as what they were: Porteath Bee Centre's tiny slice of nature in the shadow of the spectacular Eden Project; Blackgang Chine's steadfast refusal to be Disneyland; Avebury's magnificent ravaged majesty next to the neutered freak show of Stonehenge.

Many of these attractions trust you to make your own fun, free from intrusive handholding and embarrassing, proscriptive interaction. In the main, they steer well clear of excessive documentation and embellishment, just letting the exhibits or the environment speak for themselves. These places don't tell you what to think, they just tell you to think.

We make no apology that our choice of where to go and what we enjoyed there reflects our own little obsessions. Looking at the finished text, this is obviously the product of four childhoods overshadowed by the Cold War and raised by television. We also appear to have a disproportionate affection for the barely-buttoned-down insanity of the Victorians. Not everyone will get the same satisfaction from these attractions as we did. Too right. This is the antithesis of one-size-fits-all entertainment.

Doubtless we've barely scratched the surface of what's out there – these are hidden gems, so dozens of great examples will have slipped under our radar. We wanted to pass on our general enthusiasm, not devise a strict itinerary. All the attractions were tested afterwards for anecdotal value in strenuous real-pub conditions, and they make great yarns. There must be plenty more of these frontline tourist tales to gather, reflecting different tastes within the national palate, and we hope this book might inspire readers to explore further.

Although it's good to report that the year we spent writing this book was a bumper one for British tourism, the little subset of it covered herein has suffered some terrible recent losses. We tried in vain to track down a terrific-sounding collection of cinema organs that had died with its owner (much to the sadness of the local tourist board). We started writing an entry on a museum of packaging and ephemera we had visited in Wigan only to find out that the collection was about to shut up shop and be packed into crates. We would have loved to share the delights of Potter's Museum of Curiosities at the Jamaica Inn in Cornwall, a 150-year-old taxidermy exhibit, which included a stuffed kitten wedding and a monkey riding a goat, but this startling collection has now been split up, auctioned off and will probably never be seen together in one place again. Don't even get us started on the untimely demise of the bar in Southwark where you could be served cocktails by a wisecracking robot. It's too upsetting.

Despite these small black clouds, the real joy of making this book was meeting the men and women who care for these attractions. Some are struggling to make ends meet, but they all shared their time and enthusiasm. Delightfully, we were asked by several owners and curators to assure them that they would be depicted as eccentrics – their bloody-minded persistence at the fringes of tourism worn as a badge of honour. We laughed a lot making this book, and that was often thanks to the absurd, occasionally black sense of humour of those we met. The people behind these Uncommonly British attractions turned out to be the very definition of Britishness,* at least the bit of it that relies on politeness, enthusiasm, humour, charm, intelligence and liberality.

So, we say Bollocks to Alton Towers. If you prefer going round a rollercoaster at a hundred miles an hour with ice cream in your hair, fair enough. We'll be in a field elsewhere, pottering quietly amid broken bits of Gloster Gladiator.† There are, as admission figures prove, enough thrill-seekers in Britain to keep Alton Towers and its friends going quite happily for years to come. Most of the people who keep these theme parks in business, we're sure, would be bored silly spending a day in Oxford, noses pressed against a dense, dusty, dark little glass cabinet full of swazzles and mouth organs, or wandering pointlessly round

---

*In 2004, a MORI Poll for the RSA asked people all over the world, from Mumbai to King's Lynn, to define what 'Britishness' meant to them. Our national character was summed up with these key words: humour, politeness, reserve, individuality, pride and tradition; a list that might well be engraved above the lintel of the British Lawnmower Museum.

†If this appeals, we recommend the RAF Trust at Brenzett in East Sussex, where volunteers have scoured Romney Marsh for the remaining fragments of the aircraft that fell out of the sky during the Battle of Britain. It's smashing.

the backstreets of Borehamwood peering over fences at nothing. That's fine. We aren't going to stop you. To each their own. That is the British way.

But if you do fancy something out of the ordinary, something that delivers a more slowly burning pleasure, and takes a little effort and imagination, try the sort of thing we've recommended in this book. Remember, all tourist attractions depend on public interest, and the slice of the public to which these ones appeal is often necessarily narrow. So if you like the look of somewhere, go. If you don't, who will?

Oh, and don't forget to take an umbrella. We've never seen rain like it.

A Note on the Photographs

Barring a couple of exceptions where indoor photography was prohibited to the public or officially licensed photos were all that were permitted for publication, all the pictures in this book were taken by us during our visits. If something can only be seen on the horizon, we have a picture of it on the horizon. If it's so dark in there that you might as well be blindfolded, the photographs reflect that. The brochures for an attraction may feature professionally taken postcard-shots showing the gloomy Great Hall in perfect studio lighting, but that hasn't happened here.

Similarly, though sometimes a family photo album will have, amongst the muted images of children in cagoules scurrying through grey rubble, an aerial view of a whole castle in suspiciously crisp colour with a moat the colour of Domestos, we have not cheated by buying our memories wholesale from the giftshop. We no more approve of this practice than we do the use of wood glue to impersonate milk on cereal box photography.

The pictures in this book are, where possible, proper holiday snaps. We have, however, left out the ones with our thumbs in the way.

Blackgang Chine

Anything for a quiet life.

Thomas Middleton

Blackgang Chine – a resolutely old-fashioned pleasure garden cut from the cliffs of the Isle of Wight – is Britain's oldest theme park. While others have since sprung up nationwide, all increasingly successful at aping the slick presentation and nail-biting thrills of their American prototypes, Blackgang Chine stands as a reminder of how a theme park could be if we'd gone our own way. It's a duckbilled platypus – part of an abandoned evolutionary line of theme parks built for the more modest tastes of the British palate. This is what Disneyland might have looked like had the blueprints been drawn up by Enid Blyton.

Victorian hairdressing entrepreneur Alexander Dabell is the man we have to thank for Blackgang. In the 1840s, he bought the Chine ('chink' or 'cleft,' crossword enthusiasts) and sculpted the rugged cliffside into a promenade garden for the enjoyment and invigoration of holidaying ladies and gentlemen. In 1842, following a lucky beaching and a lot of boiling of bones, he was able to add a whale in a shed. And, apart from the installation of some wobbly mirrors and a model village, this seems to have been enough to keep the punters queuing up for more than a century.

Then, in 1967, Dabell's great grandson visited America and came back with a new plan – Blackgang Chine was going to take on Disney at his own game.

Though we do often swoon at the merest hint of Yankee pizzazz and adopt Americanisms without a fight, casting our cricket pads aside to hang about at the malt shop eating pastrami on rye, there is also an honourable British tradition of taking the best America can offer and twisting it bloody-mindedly to fit our own culture. In the 1930s, for example, British newspapers redrew *Superman* strips to remove The Man of Steel's ludicrous American muscles and make him look less like an alien walking amongst mortals and more like a retired wrestler who'd let himself go. Not so much 'faster than a speeding bullet,' more 'quick as a wheelbarrow'.

In this spirit, Dick Dabell recreated Disneyland on the Isle of Wight in a reasonable, affable guise with smart shoes, a centre parting and lashings of ginger beer. Blackgang takes the theme park, with all its howling and squealing and hullabaloo, and has a stiff word with it, explaining calmly that it's making a scene and everybody's staring.

In modern theme parks, the aim is always to seek the extreme – every attraction must be the fastest, the highest, the most sickening, the flashiest, the most spectacular. This, fairly obviously, goes against every fibre of the British national character, stomping clumsily over our preference for the modest and the understated. When we do try to join in, thirsting for thrills, we just look clunky, ungainly, inappropriate. A British theme park screaming that it's the quickest and the best is a faintly embarrassing spectacle, like a geography teacher bodypopping in a cowboy hat.

We ought to face facts. We don't do big, heart-stopping stunts very well. That's what Hollywood and Las Vegas are for. A few decades back, while an American in a stars-and-stripes cape was levelling the nose-cone of his rocket cycle at the opposite side of the Grand Canyon, the daredevils on this side of the Atlantic were content to jump a couple of red buses on a bike that looked like it had been recently unbolted from its sidecar.

If we were forced to choose a national fairground ride, it would probably be the Waltzer. The Waltzer is not extreme in any way. It's reasonably speedy, reasonably disorientating, and it requires no computer-controlled stress testing by Californian Professors of Rollercoasternautics to set one up on a village green, making do with a saloon bar's worth of burly men with spanners. At the end of the ride you are reasonably excited and feel reasonably sick. The only ride as British as the Waltzer is that one where children sit in gently rotating teacups, waving. Naturally, Blackgang Chine has one of those.

So, apart from the cups, what does Blackgang Chine have if it doesn't have machines for throwing you against the ground so fast that you bite your eyebrows? Well, there are some pleasant walks, and some models of things. There are several carefully built little worlds designed to spark children's imaginations, based on traditional favourites such as cowboys, dinosaurs and fairy tales. Nothing makes too much noise. Nothing is the biggest in the world. Nothing clatters very fast overhead full of overexcited teenagers and drops vomit onto you.

Most importantly of all, no ghastly animal mascot with big velour feet will tell you to have a nice day. If there's one thing the British love it's being left well alone to get on with whatever it is they're doing. So you can have a perfectly rotten day if you like. A real stinker. You can sit grumpily on top of a replica Wild West stagecoach watching your children poke each other repeatedly in the eye, and no one dressed as a giant mouse will come over and insist you all cheer up and start having a good time.

There are some concrete dinosaurs looming out of hedges at just the right points to scare anyone under ten, but surrounded by safety mats so that the older kids can ride on them. There's a gold rush town where you can have your photo taken hanging from the gallows, followed by a cup of tea and a sausage roll. There's a nursery rhyme garden where you're allowed to live out what is surely everyone's childhood fantasy of sitting on a giant mushroom pretending to be a goblin. There's a maze that anyone above four feet tall can see right over. And a collection of chimney pots. And, of course, some cavemen.

There are no switchback rides, no ticker-tape parades, no ten-minute chair massages in the conference centre health suite. It's just a beautiful cliff-top park full of statues and buildings and stuff to climb on, with no pressure. Anyone whose heart sinks at a party when they realise they are about to be press-ganged into a conga will love it. Ultimately, what makes Blackgang Chine such a lovely example of its breed is all the stuff it doesn't have. Hours of queues, for example.

Usually at a theme park, before you're allowed to climb into a coal scuttle and go at a million miles an hour upside down, you have to spend simply ages going at nought miles an hour in a line of sticky eight-year-olds who want to go wee-wees. Chessington World of Adventures even has 'How long are the queues?' as the third most important question in its publicity information, above 'How to get there?'

Of course, the British love a queue, but queuing for sensible things like a bus to the library, Centre Court tickets at Wimbledon, or bread in 1943 is a different matter entirely to queuing for a ninety-second industrial emetic. Because Blackgang Chine is about walks not rides, you can go wherever you like and take your own time, without ever feeling you're being shepherded round. You can, though it might sound an old-fashioned idea for a day out, actually relax.

Blackgang Chine is a product of a quieter, more reasonable age. It hasn't changed in decades. Not because of some preservation order slapped on the place to preserve its innate loveliness, but because it's slowly falling into the sea. Every penny earned at the turnstiles is invested in an annual battle with the crumbling cliffs on which it stands. In 1995, for example, The Wild West Town was lifted, shifted, and rebuilt wholesale a few yards further inland, exactly as it was. If things keep going on this way, in a few years, the Crooked House will be the only stable place to stand, and the entire park will probably be in Portsmouth.

The rapacious appetite of the sea has spared us anyone at the park suggesting they spend their excess profits on replacing all the displays with 400 mph swingboats or a Harry Potter centrifuge. Sadly, we do have to report that recently Blackgang Chine did introduce Water Force, a '100 metre high-speed boat slide' which, naturally, we went nowhere near. But, despite this concession to fairground fun, the new attraction is far from the focal point of the park. Water Force feels like a latecomer, a grudging tip of the hat to Blackgang's rivals. It doubtless makes commercial sense, but hopefully it isn't the first, disquieting sign of surrender.*

Though it was Britain's first example of the breed, the delight of Blackgang is how it stands apart from what the theme park has become. Where most are brash, Blackgang is modest, and where most are exhausting, Blackgang is relaxing. Tellingly, from visitors' comments, this is somewhere that people go when young, remember as magical, then bring their own children. Perhaps it's magical because, deprived of its more modern competitors' reliance on money and technology, Blackgang Chine is forced to depend on the one thing its young visitors have in spades – imagination.

---

*Since the first edition of this book was published, Blackgang has added a rollercoaster to their list of attractions, but it travels at a sensible, British 35 mph, hardly fast enough to blow off a summer boater or ruffle a moustache. As a concession to the advancing waves, the whole ride is portable.

British Lawnmower Museum

One half of the world cannot understand the pleasures of the other.

Jane Austen, *Emma*

Whenever the world becomes too much to take, whenever things seem difficult, annoying or confusing, millions of Britons take solace in sheds and garages, knowing that there is something mechanical in there, lying in bits, and it's not going to ask them any tricky questions.

Whether it's rebuilding old steam engines or tinkering with motorbike gearboxes, there's nothing

Homo Britannicus likes more than hiding behind a big pile of machine parts. We are a proud nation of enthusiast engineers, who regularly escape visits by unwanted in-laws to skulk at a workbench quietly inventing the computer, or designing a Mars probe or, here at the literal cutting edge of man-in-shed achievement, restoring one of the planet's biggest collections of vintage lawnmowers.

The British Lawnmower Museum in Southport is one of the purest, most British attractions in this book. As the curator will inform you, the lawnmower is a Great British Object. Other nations, with less luxuriant grass and less exacting standards of mowing, may claim to use lawnmowers, but look closely in their fiendish foreign sheds and chances are you'll find a 'grasscutter' (a name to be spat, not savoured). With their rotating, horizontal blades and crude slashing action, these upstart machines flail away at the lawn like a dervish, leaving split ends that would cause a cricket groundsman to mumble disagreeably and pull his cap down.

Britain on the other hand is the last outpost of the genuine lawnmower; a weighty beast with a sturdy roller and a meticulous cylinder action, snipping the grass with the delicacy of a hairdresser, and styling it into verdant stripes. The Japanese and German companies who manufacture most of the world's garden equipment nowadays grind their teeth in fury that we will not abandon our trusty mowers, since they really only make the things for us. Though we may have surrendered the Marathon bar and the Vauxhall Nova to the cause of international standardisation, we will not leave our Suffolk Punches behind. By visiting the British Lawnmower Museum, you are truly celebrating part of our national heritage.

Southport itself is rather pretty, all Victorian seaside splendour, broad, well-kept promenades and – thank God – immaculate lawns. If you've come by car, you'll have an ideal opportunity to admire the town's ornate ironwork arcades while you sit trapped in traffic in the ornate filter system in the high street. But it's worth the Herculean effort that it takes to turn left, because just behind the main drag is Stanley's Hardware, the garden shed of dreams.

Downstairs, Stanley's is a good old-fashioned British hardware shop, a family business which opened in 1945 as the area's first DIY store. But if you go up the stairs, past the waiting gnome and on to the landing, you enter lawnmower Valhalla.

The grass-look carpet is an acknowledgement that

upstairs isn't the mower's natural habitat. Nonetheless, the first-floor rooms are a tangled sea of handles, grassboxes and fuel tanks, gloriously finished in British racing green, picked out with the occasional splash of pillar-box red, and polished to a dazzling sheen with the chamois leather of love.

At first, you may be a little bemused. We are raised to understand the thrill of an aircraft hangar full of old Spitfires, or a restored locomotive, but you may not know how to react to a building full of old lawnmowers. The correct answer is with awe.

As with any display of mechanical heritage, the museum is a triumph of the restorer's art. Every model is in glorious *Flying Scotsman* repair, and where the wooden parts of the particularly antique mowers have rotted with age, they have been replaced by hand-turned pieces.

There are steam mowers, electric mowers, petrol mowers, hover mowers, racing mowers and toy mowers. There are mowers built by firms more used to making limousines (Rolls-Royce), jump jets (Hawker-Siddeley) or fire engines (Dennis). There are steel leviathans and tiny plastic prototypes, steam mowers and models designed to be drawn by elephants. There's even a two-inch wide mower, the existence of which was denied by its manufacturer when the museum called them to ask for information.

You'll emerge brimming with facts. How have you lived so long without knowing that Charles Darwin was the proud owner of a Samuelson Donkey Lawnmower? Or that the Flymo was originally blue and only changed to orange following a survey of the colour preferences of 1960s housewives? (Come to that, did you know that the prototype Flymo – and it seems obvious when you think about it – was a dustbin lid with an engine stuck to it?)

The original cylinder mower was invented in 1830 by Edwin Beard Budding as a device for trimming the bobbles off cloth for guardsmen's uniforms. Making one of those intuitive leaps that separates inventors from, say, solicitors or crabs, he converted his invention to lawn use and, after testing the machine at night to avoid having people think he was mad, Budding set about single-handedly revolutionising the British garden. He towers over this collection like a god.

You see the hallmark of the obsessive museum: endless exhibited permutations of the same-shaped thing. There are more than 200 mowers on display, from a total of almost 450 amassed over forty years, all presenting similar silhouettes against the white wall, like a string of paper dolls cut out by someone who was really into lawnmowers.

Every now and then, however, the pattern is broken by intriguing one-offs, such as the Atco Training Car. Constructed as part of a wartime programme to teach people to drive, the Training Car is just Atco's standard lawnmower with the handles removed and some Noddy-car bodywork bolted to the top. Above it hangs a picture of dozens of happy motorists, their suited and hatted top-halves poking up from their Atco dodgems, putt-putting off to a brighter future.

Most of the mowers are relics of such bygone eras, when things were built properly, and meant to last. The design classic of the collection is probably the Green's Silens Messor, the Victorian machine that kept the Empire's lawns trim. It was still being manufactured at the outbreak of the Second World War, unchanged, eighty years after it was first introduced. It's doubtful much of the modern garden equipment for sale downstairs is designed with such lengthy service in mind.

That's not to say that the museum divorces itself

from the modern world. As a goodwill gesture towards today's cult of celebrity there is a glittering line-up of star lawnmowers and garden tools. Rock fans will be excited to see Brian May's own majestic mower, and Jean Alexander (Hilda Ogden in *Coronation Street*) kindly donated her Qualcast Panther. 'Mega Star' Nicholas Parsons planned to give the museum his own lawnmower, but it was stolen, so he had to send some secateurs instead. Elsewhere Ainsley Harriott, Brian Sewell and Alan Titchmarsh have raided their sheds in the name of heritage and, if you look really carefully, you might catch a glimpse of perhaps the most unlikely museum exhibit in Britain: Joe Pasquale's strimmer.

And although 'I've Seen Joe Pasquale's Strimmer' badges are not on sale (surely they're missing a trick?) there is a perfect gift to take home in the form of the *Lawnmower World* VHS or DVD. This is an enhanced version of the live guided tour. It's billed as *The British Lawnmower Museum: The Movie* on posters round the shop, and effortlessly lives up to the hype, even going so far as to feature 'The Lawnmower Song', a country-and-western number specially written for the film by a descendant of lawnmower pioneer Edwin Beard Budding. Now you want to own it.

The film is personally introduced by curator Brian Radam with infectious enthusiasm. Brian, a lovely man who looks like a combination of three quarters of The Who, is an ex-musician and former lawn-mower racing champion whose father founded Stanley's Hardware. He worked as an apprentice for Atco while he was at school, and has forgotten more about mowers than most people will ever learn. He proudly sports a *Blue Peter* badge commemorating his on-air demonstration of some of the museum's collection, including the million pound Husqvarna Solar Mower – a cake-shaped Swedish robot grass-cutter that screams when it's stolen. This is the same Husqvarna that confused the *Blue Peter* dogs so much that they mistook it for a sheep and tried to round it up.

The British Lawnmower Museum is one of the nation's great treasures. We British are rightly proud of our lawns, which give our green and pleasant land a lot of its green-and-pleasant-ness. The lawnmower, so redolent of Sunday morning pottering in the garden and glorious sixes scored over baize-smooth cricket pitches, is one of the things that make us who we are. The preservation of our heritage depends on enthusiasts choosing to care for the corners of history that might otherwise be ignored. There's more obvious glamour in old cars or motorbikes or steam trains, but that means there are plenty of people prepared to save them from the scrapheap. The team here have shunned the comparative limelight in order to shower their love on an engineering underdog, and there's nothing more British than that.

Peasholm Park Naval Warfare

Believe me my young friend, there is NOTHING – absolutely nothing – half so much worth doing as simply messing about in boats.

Kenneth Grahame, *The Wind in the Willows*

The ancient Greeks called it *naumachia*. The Romans plumped for *navalia proelia*. We know it as Naval Warfare at Peasholm Park. And we know it as that because the fine employees of Scarborough Borough Council are the only people in Britain who care enough to keep this specialized form of military re-enactment alive.

During the summer weeks, the leisure staff of this bewitching Japanese-themed park take a working break from painting the pagoda or maintaining the laughing dragon pedaloes. To the accompaniment of a chap playing stirring wartime hits on a floating organ platform, grown men and women sit in replica ships and shoot fireworks at each other. They have been performing a rollicking half-hour mock sea battle in this former spa town since George V was kicking around – and it's unarguably the most excellent fun.

There was a time when Scarborough didn't have the *naumachia* market completely sewn up; several British parks put on this type of regular show throughout the eighteenth and nineteenth centuries. Slowly these entertainments drifted out of public favour until this relatively young pretender became the sole upholder of a noble tradition of simulated torpedoes and freshwater lakes pretending to be the Atlantic Ocean.

Tacitus wrote of similar spectacles two thousand years ago. Caesars Julius and Claudius went absolutely potty over them, although the costs involved were prohibitive. Thousands of gladiators (naturally, this was a fight to the death) would crew scaled-down triremes, attacking each other whilst legionaries unsportingly bombarded them with flaming missiles from the edge of the water-filled arenas. Claudius even spent eleven years having a hole drilled through a mountain so that he could have a reasonable excuse to hold one by way of celebration on the tunnel's completion.

George Horrocks, entertainments emperor of the Scarborough Corporation, issued a Caesar-like 1927 decree that there should be a North Yorkshire revival of this declining practice. Did Horrocks know what he was starting with this thrice-weekly piece of delightful municipal theatre?

His local punters had demonstrably not enjoyed the all-too-real naval skirmish they'd been through only a decade earlier. German battlecruisers shelled the hell out of Scarborough just a week before the first Christmas of the Great War. To add insult to fatalities, the town's lighthouse and medieval castle both sustained serious damage.

Many of those watching in the early years of the show would have been able to remember that traumatic Sunday morning of 1914. Now they could revel in a mildly cathartic revenge as models of Fritz's dreadnoughts and U-boats were sent packing. The second outbreak of global hostilities twelve years later caused the only hiatus in Peasholm Park's rather more genteel variety of warfare. Again, Scarborough failed to escape the firepower of the Fatherland, and was bombed during the Battle of Britain.

Where the Luftwaffe had failed to destroy Peasholm's miniature maritime heroes in World War Two, woodworm succeeded. Dry rot had also set in and a replacement fleet had to be ordered. By the time the display made its triumphant return it was based on the Allied victory at the Battle of the River Plate, with HMS *Ajax*, *Achilles*, and *Exeter* taking centre lake opposite the *Admiral Graf Spee*.

With just a few minor tweaks, Peasholm's admirals have remained faithful to the same script ever since. In 1960 a cute wire-mounted RAF began to carry out successful air strikes on the enemy in retaliation for Scarborough's Second World War battering. The mini-planes entered the fray over the heads of a gasping audience long before George Lucas stole the idea for the opening sequence of *Star Wars*. Finally any reference to the identities of the participating navies was quietly dropped and it became a simple matter of a brave flotilla defending itself against an anonymous aggressor. Although the famous British names are still in use, the *Graf Spee* has become the *Robert Eaves*, after an unlucky former warden at Peasholm. A story as strong as this needs no embellishment, and nowadays no one feels the need to mention the war.

On a performance day the key staff start their twelve-hour shift at 6 a.m., rowing out to the central island to inspect the boats and shoo away the nosey ducks. The park begins to fill up an hour-and-a-half before battle commences; expectant holidaymakers and cheery regulars of all ages grab themselves prime viewing spots on the amphitheatre seating for the forthcoming treat.*

The genial master of ceremonies eases the spectators into the mood with a selection of popular organ favourites prior to an infectious bout of audience participation with 'If You're Happy and You Know It'. Do I have to clap my hands and stamp my feet? Yes. Otherwise your cheers and boos and oohs and aahs won't sound right. Despite yourself, your precious national reticence quickly evaporates as the

---

*Don't underestimate this. Even though we went to the penultimate performance of the season it was standing or squatting room only for latecomers.

joyous pantomime of the show hits all the right buttons.

To the strains of what else but 'Sailing', the car-battery-powered merchant ships pull into view. A bullying battleship has a brazen pop at them; our heroic boys launch a spirited and decisive assault in return. Nerve-shredding cracks and bangs, billowing smoke, the noisy tears of the less hardy toddler, this naval warfare lark has got it all. There's even an appearance from the *Ark Royal*.

The aircraft carrier is the oldest vessel currently in use at Peasholm Park, dating back to the mid-1970s. It's done well considering that most of them manage twenty to twenty-five years' service at best until a firm in Whitby is contracted to build a replacement. One no longer lakeworthy craft is seeing out its retirement usefully by playing a target hulk in the enemy naval base. And may we pray a moment's silence for the unfortunate *Achilles*, which recently stunned the participants more than the onlookers when it unexpectedly sank in a narrative non-sequitur, requiring a dramatic mid-performance rescue.

Whether or not any extra unscheduled excitement such as this occurs, when the several captains remove the lids of these twenty-feet-long pyrotechnical beasts to pop their heads out and wave at you, they have earned that ringing applause. These aren't wide-eyed obsessives, they've just got the best job in the world. Floating, motorised Cowboys and Indians. The queue of families waiting patiently afterwards to stage their own battles in the pedaloes and rowing boats is testament enough to the efforts of the staff.

The Peasholm Park Naval Warfare is unique, genuinely impressive and refreshingly free of cynicism. The £300,000 grant received in late 2004 from the Heritage Lottery Fund is well deserved and will help significantly towards restoring the park to its landscaped best. They're doing all this to entertain you. Get out there and be entertained. Caesar has commanded you.

Louis Tussaud's House of Wax

*Wax-works weren't made to be looked at for nothing.
Nohow!*

Lewis Carroll, *Throuyh the Looking Glass*

'Wax (don't) works' screamed the clueless
headline in the *Daily Mirror* on the 13th
November, 2003. 'We reveal Britain's worst, and we
mean worst, museum,' continued the ditsy showbiz
columnist, who'd obviously had one too few junkets
in her diary that week. Of course, the newspaper,
bless its cheap little heart, wasn't actually revealing
anything: the piece was a re-hash of a 'FW: FW: FW:

25

FW: youll luv this!!?!' e-mail that had been doing the rounds for the previous three days.

Some wag had turned up at Louis Tussaud's, snapped a few pictures, and turned them into a parlour game. The idea was to guess the celebrity from the photo of their wax likeness. The joke was that the waxworks weren't really very good.

But why single out Great Yarmouth's House of Wax from countless other waxworks museums around Britain? Although a surprising number of mad people seem to want to queue for hours to get into Madame Tussaud's in London, it must be understood that most of these places are a waste of time and should be avoided if at all possible.

Three-dimensional wax likenesses may once have provided an exciting opportunity for the public to meet shiny versions of the rich and famous, but celebrities are almost unavoidable these days, on the TV, the radio, in what used to be newspapers. It seems unlikely that, as a nation, we get the same thrill from seeing stars that we once did. We're now so used to celebs sneaking into our daily life that we wouldn't blink if, on cracking open a freshly boiled egg, we saw Simon Cowell's smug face etched in the yolk.

And fame-hounds these days demand so much more than a wax lookalike to get their celebrity fix. They want to know where the celebs live, which diet regime they follow and with whom they've been most recently spotted sunbathing. Magazines have sprung up to quench this thirst with a carefully controlled leak of celebrity-approved 'gossip'. Or, if that's not enough, there are reality television shows where half-forgotten has-beens clamber gracelessly back into the public consciousness by eating buckets of ants or getting pecked by ostriches. Against this unavoidable blizzard of carefully managed public relations propaganda, a wax statue that looks vaguely like someone off the telly isn't really going to cut the mustard.

The main argument for visiting the £22-a-go Madame Tussaud's in London has always been that the models are so lifelike. As the world's most famous waxworks museum, of course, Madame Tussaud's has the stars lining up to be immortalised. Public figures will sit happily for hours on end slathered in uncomfortable face-moulds to give the sculptor plenty of reference material. Even casts of their hands will be taken to ensure every aspect of their costly manicure is captured in perfect detail. It's a publicist's dream.

Now that celebrities no longer just push other people's brands – being a brand themselves – a high-profile waxwork can be a part of their carefully maintained self-image. So, as if standing excitedly next to something that isn't George Clooney wasn't a ludicrous enough way to spend the day, the punters in London are essentially queuing up to visit a collection of hugely expensive adverts. Doesn't that make you feel dirty? (If it doesn't, Madame Tussaud's publicity material – 'squeeze Brad's bum . . . make J-Lo blush' – should come in handy.)

Louis Tussaud's House of Wax in Great Yarmouth is a much more down-to-earth affair. Unlike his great grandmother's high-profile attraction in the capital, Louis' waxworks has no confused, mile-long queues of Swedish backpackers waiting to get inside and not know who Des Lynam is. The museum's double-bayed Victorian house sits quietly back from the discount gonk emporia and comedy noise shops of Regent Road, a cascade of hand-painted signboards the only visible concession to tacky seaside bluster.

One, propped up by the entrance, attempts an explanation: 'Waxworks are more enjoyable if it is remembered that they are 'snapshots' taken in wax at the high point of their fame.' It's a neat excuse for not having updated the exhibits in fifteen years, and presumably saves them the chore of having to change Michael Jackson's nose and David Beckham's hair every week. It's what makes the Yarmouth waxworks so special. Rather than a voguish slice of who's hot and who's not, we have a museum commemorating those celebrities who have made an impression on visitors to Great Yarmouth over the years. Why go to Madame Tussaud's and see Christina Aguilera and Michael Jordan when they're plastered all over the newspapers already? But how long is it since you've had a really close look at Max Boyce and Ian Botham?

Yet people sneer. Perhaps it's because the standard of sculpture has been set impossibly high by Madame Tussaud's celebrity-endorsed replicas (the chances of Clint Eastwood popping in for a sitting in Great Yarmouth are pretty low). But it's also because the choice of stars at Yarmouth reflects a Britain that has now gone. Frankly it looks a little primitive and parochial for today's globally attuned tastes, which is what makes it interesting.

This House of Wax is preserved at that point in time, not so long ago, when Cannon and Ball were the nation's top entertainers and everyone in the country stayed in at the weekend to watch Saturday night television. There are concessions to comparatively recent figures, such as Gorden Kaye and the Paul Gascoigne formerly known as Gazza, but essentially the House of Wax stands as a living tribute to old Variety Show Britain, a trip back to the days when holidaymakers headed for the nation's coast and stopped there, and to the stars they loved.

Of course the makers found space to erect statues of Jim Davidson, Michael Barrymore and Noel Edmonds (complete with an uncannily accurate waxwork Mr Blobby) – these are the celebrities whose fans built Britain's seaside towns. Whilst the last surviving breeding pair of Grumbleweeds perform on the Great Yarmouth pier next to a bar decorated with wooden paintings of Su Pollard and Russ Abbot, the museum will continue to reflect the tastes of the traditional British seaside-visiting public.

The inclusion of a hall of mirrors, table football and fantastic mid-1970s amusement arcade (complete with a 10p-a-go Rifle Range and funky looking *Travel Time* pinball machine) just reinforces the impression that this is The Attraction That Modern Culture Forgot. The whole experience is a time machine – you are an eight-year-old visiting the seaside with your nan. It costs about the same as it did then, too.

Go round the waxworks realising that they can little afford to update the models, let alone pay for top celebrity sittings and it all begins to make a bit more sense. Local sculptors have actually attempted to model these stars from scratch (and by the looks of it, in some cases from memory). There's no cheating here. The clothes aren't expensive duplicates donated by the same fashion house that supplied the original, but hand-tailored approximations. Kylie looks great in a car coat, and Barry Manilow's peach Debenhams sale jumper fits the man particularly well.

But it's not just teatime favourites in casual wear. Louis Tussaud has his own Chamber of Horrors, just like the one his Great Grandma built. Descend some steps into half darkness and come face to face with murderers such as John Christie, Charles Manson and Peter Sutcliffe. (Leslie Grantham is upstairs.) It makes you wonder at what point killers earn themselves a waxy place in the nation's hearts. All waxworks become numb to good taste at this point; the proud puff for London's Madame Tussaud's includes the confusing promise that there's 'more than live serial killers in our chamber' (has anyone told Health and Safety?) and avers that wandering amongst restaged acid bath murders and the like is 'great gruesome fun.' No doubt there would be voices of dissent at the first waxworks to include a great gruesome fun Fred and Rose West before their despicable crimes have become acceptably colourful social history.

Like its jolly collection of mass murderers, the Yarmouth waxworks have become undoubtedly more famous since their 'bad' publicity. The other Louis Tussaud's wax museum in Blackpool may have a lot more money at its disposal (and a Robbie Williams) but it has only received a fraction of the coverage afforded its humbler cousin. It would also be fair to suggest that Tussaud's of Yarmouth has hogged more recent column inches than its grander London namesake, too. Good. We can only hope that any influx of money from its newfound fame doesn't go towards filling rooms with Eminems and Rooneys.

Approached in the right frame of mind, Louis Tussaud's House of Wax isn't just a collection of waxworks, it's a collection preserved in aspic: a museum of variety, a celebration of the fickle nature of fame (ooh, look, it's John Forsyth and Barry Sheene, and he's got a finger missing) and perhaps even a museum of itself. A stroll round it is like coming across a dusty newspaper at the back of a wardrobe and indulging yourself in its gossip columns, sports pages or television listings. It's a trip down a modestly short memory lane, and the longer it stands, the longer grows the lane. Rather than attempt to keep up with the considerably wealthier Joneses, with their waxwork Andrex puppy* (for God's sake) this is a museum showing how and who we used to idolise. And as the lifespan of fame shortens ever further and the definition of celebrity grows ever flabbier, this is a strangely timely traditional British seaside experience, wax warts and all.

*Yes, there's one at Madame T's. It won a public vote as the Most Popular Fictional Television Character, which deserves some kind of bloody explanation.

Kelvedon Nuclear Bunker

Were one half of mankind brave and one half cowards,
the brave would be always beating the cowards. Were
all brave, they would lead a very uneasy life; all would
be continually fighting: but being all cowards, we go
on very well.

Samuel Johnson, *The Life of Samuel Johnson*
by James Boswell

Because they're big, vain and splendid, castles are always popular with tourists. Nerve centres for the powerful, they are built on a grand scale, able to withstand the most devastating weapons of their time. Castles are also a handy way to keep the angry plebs at bay – the first thing the nobs did during the Peasants' Revolt was hide in the Tower of London. So of course, if you're after a castle, you can have a very British day out at the Tower, shuffling past a lot of vulgar jewellery in the dark and feeling werry umble indeed. But if you want a castle with a twist, consider the twentieth-century equivalent in Essex instead.

The Secret Nuclear Bunker at Kelvedon Hatch easily qualifies as The World's Most Terrifying Bungalow. It's a place made all the more extraordinary for its very ordinary setting, on a country lane between Chipping Ongar, once the furthest outpost of the Central Line, and Brentwood, infamously crowned the Most Boring Town in Britain. At first sight an unremarkable 1950s farm cottage, this bungalow is in fact the tip of a government iceberg – a huge, three-storey bunker with 10ft thick concrete walls reaching 100ft underground. The local villagers knew nothing of its purpose, being the sort of people who could, back in 1952, remain unfazed by 40,000 tons of cement trundling up the road to Parrish Farm. Even the contractors weren't told what they were building.

35

This is where the select few government leaders, military commanders and civil servants would have been whisked twenty miles from London to run the country in the event of a nuclear strike. As many as 600 'key personnel' would have lived and worked in the bunker for a minimum of three months without venturing outside. You'd be safe here in the event of a nuclear winter, making it the most all-weather tourist attraction in Britain. Even Center Parcs can't compete with that.

Walk through the front door of the bungalow, and you enter a world where the clocks strike thirteen. There's nobody in a customised baseball cap to take your money*. There's nobody there at all. Atmosphere comes before commerce. You're utterly alone. Past a steel cage and locked door marked 'Decontamination Unit – Dirty Area' you descend a handful of steps and find yourself at one end of a 350ft tunnel. Suddenly it's freezing. At the other end is a pair of one-and-a-half ton blast doors made of tank metal. Whoever built this place wasn't joking.

By now, your mobile phone will have cut out.

*There is an honesty box at the exit. You have to pay to get out.

You're walking into a Faraday cage – the MI6 building at Vauxhall Cross has one – where radio signals are kept at bay. Echoes bounce off the cold walls: sirens and static from a crackling PA system. Something has happened. The place is alive with fear.

The three-tier bunks that line the walls would have been used as crushable blast protection in an emergency, and the tunnel's length would have made it easy to pick off intruders. And which visitors would they have wanted to shoot in the days following a nuclear strike? Unfortunately, the unpalatable answer is you. Imagine all the people you'd voted for running away while your country went up in smoke. If you discovered them a few days later, hiding in a hill in Essex, you'd want a quiet word. Sadly, they'd shoot you before you trod any of that nasty radiation in on your shoes.

The blast tunnel has two L-bends in it for extra protection and is raked imperceptibly downwards to the enormous three-storey Regional Government Headquarters. As you stand at the far end looking up a staircase into the gloom, it's hard to comprehend how you've suddenly ended up about eighty feet underground. You're actually deep within a hill, on the Bunker's lowest and most secure level. Here are housed the plant and communications network, including a soundproofed BBC studio to transmit reassuring, familiar voices to what remained of the nation.

This is a grim exercise in the art of belt and braces; a bureaucratic response to the unthinkable. The assumption is that survival depends upon never going outside. Your resources are limited: you can't flush the toilet, because that would waste some of the 24,000 gallons of stored water, so there are chemical loos. Fresh food is perishable and there isn't enough room for freezers, so you eat dry stuff and tinned things. You can't open the window and it's going to get sweaty down there with the heat of 600 human bodies and tons of equipment, so the air is cooled, cleaned, scrubbed, de-humidified and recirculated every two minutes. It's been planned like a space mission, yet all these mechanical and logistical efforts don't make you feel particularly safe, especially with all the 'Danger' and 'Do Not Enter' signs glaring at you. You get the feeling that if the lights suddenly went out, you might very well embarrass your trousers.

Upstairs, there's a planning room, from where aircraft and nuclear pollution would have been tracked. There's a huge mess kitchen and canteen, washrooms, desk space for representatives from every level of government, and dormitories. The Prime Minister's dorm is occupied by a dummy of John Major – the last PM who might possibly have been evacuated here – lying supine in bed. His eyes and mouth are wide open, giving him the air of a man kept awake by troublesome nightmares.

'Availability and Allocation of Surviving Resources,' screams one sobering chart. In other words, what's left and who gets it ('Min Ag. Fish & Fd' – cometh the horror, cometh the man from the Ministry). Telephones ring on and off, amid the constant chatter of the PA system, relaying dispassionate announcements of a five-megaton blast in north London and wind directions for fallout. The ceilings are cluttered with ducting and vents, bringing down the headroom to an oppressive level. The 1967 target list for the UK lists Catterick, Salcombe, Kidderminster – a roll-call of the ordinary in line for the terrible.

The Bunker exudes confidence in the triumph of dull toil. Government policy appears to have been 'at the moment of the unthinkable, keep yourself busy'. According to the ludicrous *Protect and Survive* pamphlet which would have been distributed seventy-two hours before an anticipated nuclear attack, on hearing the four-minute warning, Joe Public was expected to do the following: extinguish his cigarette, turn off gas, electricity and water, tape up the handles of the lavatory cistern, fill his bath with water and cover it with a door, ensure he had enough tinned food and water to last fourteen days, and retire with his portable radio, torch, blankets, tin opener, bucket, first aid kit, box of dry sand (for cleaning crockery), notebook, pencils, cleaning materials, toys, magazines, clock, calendar, wife and children to the Inner Refuge he had constructed from mattresses, tables, bags of clothing, books and heavy furniture. It was a good way of ensuring Britain was fussing about safely indoors rather than running out into the street screaming 'we're all going to fry' or robbing banks or attempting sexual intercourse with that dishy type over the road, or whatever it is that people say they'd do if they knew the world was coming to an end.

Life in the Bunker would have been a psychologically appalling privilege. If anything went wrong down here, you were unlikely to be found or helped. The audio tour of Kelvedon (highly recommended) calls it 'a concrete coffin' and it could well have turned out that way for the inhabitants. Wherever you wander, you're never far from the mortuary. The Commanding Officer even slept next to it. If you died on the job, your corpse would have been double-bagged, put in a self-assembly cardboard coffin and tossed outside to join the five to ten million others.

The central ops room has walls covered in what look like illustrations from *Look and Learn*. They show typical British high streets before and after different sorts of bomb hit them - cosy images of traditional small-town life rendered awful, as if an Ealing comedy had been blown to smithereens. Things start to look worryingly old-fashioned, as you survey vintage teleprinters and clunky mechanical phone exchanges. You are put in mind of the Cabinet War Rooms – Kelvedon's retired uncle from London – yet this is more unnerving than anything similar from World War II. We won that one, so it's not too scary that we did it using Bakelite and sensible moustaches. This place on the other hand was built for a war we still haven't fought – a vague war based on a fear that at some point someone, somewhere, would make us all hide under the ground. And we were going to defend ourselves with all this old junk, as naively as the generals of the First World War sending the cavalry into battle against machine guns.

This bleakness of tone is inevitable, but surprisingly, the Bunker has a terrific sense of black humour. As owner Mike Parrish will attest, he doesn't want to scare the shit out of people. (Look out for him, by the way: he's the one with the unmistakable smile of a man who owns a nuclear bunker.) The place may be a post-apocalyptic *Marie Celeste*, but it's scattered with dark wit. The clocks have stopped. The *Protect And Survive* manual has 'Office Copy – Do Not Remove' scrawled across it in marker pen. You can buy a souvenir jar of Bramley apple and mint relish with a radiation warning symbol on it. Every sheet of toilet paper in the washroom is stamped 'Government Property – Use Both Sides.' (Parrish does this personally – about 20 sheets a week, because people nick them.)

Kelvedon was decommissioned in 1992, when Parrish, whose family have farmed the surrounding land for generations, bought it back from the government for an undisclosed sum. They beat off bids from rivals wanting to convert it to a document store, a huge wine cellar, a pistol range or (whoops) a religious retreat. When the Parrish clan first arrived on the premises, they found the floors polished to within an inch of their lives and the grass clipped to nail-scissor perfection. The four bored guards who had been stationed there had made the place nice and tidy and nicer and tidier until it was the nicest and tidiest place for miles. It was also still on alert, as Parrish found out when an errant nephew accidentally set off a fire alarm at a New Year's Eve party. In minutes, the bunker was surrounded by police, unaware it had been decommissioned.

Of course, as a sign reminds you, the Bunker could still be re-activated. But it's unlikely, given that if Parrish decided not to surrender it, he could simply load a shotgun and lock himself in along with the *Schindler's List* of friends and family who get a safe place to hide. You can join him if you cough up £30,000 for a ten-year reservation.

Presumably the powers that be have a bigger and better bolthole now. Actually, we know they do. The Wiltshire town of Corsham 'may' (i.e. does) house Hawthorn, the 'mother of all bunkers', which should have remained a well-kept secret, except that the government sold some of it off, rather giving the game away.

Perhaps we'll be able to visit Hawthorn by 2032.

In the meantime, Kelvedon Bunker is a thrilling piece of history, a blend of the terrifying and the banal, of Geiger counters and boxes of 1000 Stationery Office No 123 Wire Staples, Coppered and Chisel Pointed for Vanguard Nos 1–4 Stapling Machines.

But was it any use? In four decades of active service, at a cost of £3m per year, Kelvedon Bunker was never at red alert status. It was, only once, cranked up to amber. Not, as you might think, during the Cuban missile crisis (which apparently happened too quickly) or the occupation of the Palestinian territories, or the invasion of Afghanistan. Kelvedon was readied for action during the 1984–85 miners' strike, when the government was concerned that the country might be on the brink of civil war. Makes you proud to be British, doesn't it?

Porteath Bee Centre

*Won't you come into my garden? I would like my roses
to see you.*

Richard Brinsley Sheridan, attrib.

J ust a few miles north of Cornwall's star turn, The
Eden Project, is an altogether more modest honey-
pot for nature-loving tourists. The Porteath Bee
Centre is an exhibition, a small business, a shop and
café for local produce all rolled into one. Endearingly
cute on the surface, there is a steelier side to this
unassuming home for the tinier creature.

When Porteath apiarists Heather Jago and Eddie

Old say that it's been a terrible summer they're not indulging in the usual polite small talk about inclement weather, or even their unEdenesque inability to control their local climate. Britain's bees are under attack from an unpleasantly sturdy parasite – the varroa – and the voracious mite is all over the West Country like a biblical plague.

It's not the humble bumble that these little buggers go after, it's your sweet tooth's best friend – the honeybee. The blood-supping scourge has been making a proper nuisance of itself throughout Europe ever since the mid-1970s but has received the barest minimum of news coverage. Perhaps if the situation had a catchy foot-and-mouth style moniker (antenna-and-proboscis?) then it might have grabbed a headline or two by now. Porteath's parasite summer has been so terrible that they, like many other honey-makers, have lost whole hives to paralysing infestations of varroa.

If that weren't dispiriting enough, the poor old *apis mellifera* finds itself on the receiving end of yet more grief when the wasps roll up for a rumble – especially in the numbers that they did in 2004. The stereotypical skinhead of the insect world, the wasp muscles its way inside hives and gets half-cut on as much honey as possible, pausing only to beat up any bees that dare to get in its way.

What is the point of wasps? Eddie sighs, wishing he knew. He's convinced that they must have some sort of a purpose but he's not at all sure what it might be. Any wasp reading this would be well advised to follow the example of the bee, and have a think about producing a sweetmeat for our toast. A nice breakfast marmalade would be ideal. Then we might stop trying to swat you all the time.

Despite facing the worst nature can throw at them, the bees and their keepers display commendably stiff upper lips. Well, the stoical keepers do anyway; it's often tricky to tell with those damned inscrutable bees.

Whoever chose the bulldog as Britain's animal mascot obviously didn't take time to consider all the options. Why is our national character best encapsulated in a wheezing, dawdling, stubborn-faced, flatulent bag of wrinkles when it could have been better embodied by a hard-working loyalist with a courageous do-or-die attitude and a funky colour scheme? It's all Winston Churchill's fault for not looking more like a bee.

From 200 or so hives, stretching across the north

of Cornwall from Port Isaac to St Agnes, the surviving Porteath-managed bees have put in some serious overtime to maintain the honey supply. The shop at the Centre has gallons of jam, mustard, fudge and mead for sale, all made using honey with nectar collected from local heather, blackberries, dandelion, hawthorn, apples and clover. There's practically a hedgerow in every jar.

Recent European legislation has dictated that the Bee Centre's jars of honey are stamped with use-by dates at least seven years distant. Without wishing to appear rabidly Eurosceptic, did Brussels not study Howard Carter's tomb raiding when it went to school? Honey stored in airtight Egyptian containers during the rule of the pharaohs was still deliciously edible when it was opened more than two and a half millennia later. The fact that honey is everlasting should come as no surprise to us because, as we all know, bees are magic. Amazingly, science has never been able to replicate the precise process that the furry fellers use to make the stuff; it's a closely guarded bee trade secret.

If humans can't make honey, then at least they can help collect it. Porteath's beekeepers prefer to retrieve honey from the hives between 11am and 2pm – the time of day when the greatest percentage of bees is out at work. Beekeepers, like burglars, have to case the joint first – there's no point in breaking and entering if everyone's at home. The bees don't seem to mind getting robbed too much, judging by the way that they hang around the Centre's van like dogs waiting to greet their returning owner.

Porteath prefer to tend their charges without the use of protective gloves so that they can 'feel the bees'. They adopt a similarly gentle approach with visitors to the Centre; without being intrusive you are subtly encouraged to learn by asking questions. These are proper interactive staff. The many effusive letters on display from children attest to the efficacy of this approach; thanks are offered for the memorable school trips spent learning all about skeps,* propolis,† and being taught how to make beeswax candles.‡

Don't be afraid to ask questions, or you'll never

---

*Old-fashioned straw hives (see the entry on the Pack O'Cards Inn).

†The resin collected to construct honeycomb. Very good for ulcers, apparently.

‡Which smell very tasty indeed.

find out that your average bee shouldn't be considered male or female – it's either a drone or a worker. Or that baby bees are fed the rather wonderful sounding bee bread. And most excitingly of all, and something that should really be taught as part of the National Curriculum: 'How to deal with a bee sting'. After your clumsy skin rips the pointy bit of the bee's arse away from its body, and your unwilling assailant buzzes off to its futile death, the best thing to do is lightly flick the sting out. Don't try and pull it, it's still full of poison and you'll only pump more into yourself. Which is no less than you deserve, you callous murderer. Why were there no public information films about that?

They're proper martyrs, bees. If they aren't dying from parasites or wasp attack or from losing their bottoms in fights with humans, then it might well be from shagging. The queen bee kills her sexual partners by tearing off their reproductive equipment once she's had her wicked way with them, avoiding any awkward fussing about when might be a polite time to phone for another date.

More information than you can shake a sticky stick at can be absorbed upstairs in the museum. An Australian educational video about bees runs on a twenty minute loop, in which Phil Simon, an antipodean Attenborough-in-waiting, helpfully reveals an encyclopaedic knowledge of his buzzy, fuzzy friends accompanied by unsettling early 1980s synthesised bee music.

Whilst holding half a pound of the stripy insects in his hands, our small-screen guide tells us, 'of course, the honeybee is *not* native to Australia'. Having been introduced down under in the early nineteenth century, they're about as Australian as Phil's forefathers were when they swanned off the boat in irons. Being tutored on bee lore by an Aussie is like turning on the cricket and finding it's being commentated by the Swiss. Our man does redeem himself by showing us some splendid footage of two queens having a bitchfight and of a knackered-out worker bee with frayed wings walking away to die gracefully. Very poignant.

One of the simplest and most pleasurable aspects of the Porteath Bee Centre, however, is that it gives you the chance to observe a load of bees going about their business. Glass-fronted display cabinets in the walls lead out into the open air and keep the humming throng at sting's length. They happily occupy themselves behind the glass, darting around specially

provided postboxes and hollow logs, totally unin-
hibited by our simple viewing pleasure. It's extremely
therapeutic, producing the kind of soothing, hypnotic effect that makes aquariums so popular. Turn
on, tune in, think bee.

So should you ever find yourself in the mood for
visiting an endangered part of the natural world on
your way through Cornwall – that most touristy
of British counties – and you don't fancy a warm
temperate biome full of homesick chunks of Malay-
sian rainforest and South African desert, make a
bee-line for Porteath instead. Support your local bee
centre.

Mad Jack's Sugar Loaf

England – a happy land we know
Where follies naturally grow

Charles Churchill, *The Ghost*

Nothing sticks two fingers up at the pernicious world of time and motion studies, marketing department reports, focus groups, efficiency graphs and feasibility projections better than the erection of an expensive structure of no possible use. Follies are excesses of high spirits preserved in brick and stone, passing fancies rendered solid. Keith Moon – the late drummer of The Who, and a fine English eccentric of recent vintage – having got bored of wantonly destroying hotel suites, used to fill his suitcases with bricks and mortar so he could leave some kind of annoyingly permanent edifice on the carpet. The staff would come in to clean his room, fearing the worst, and discover not a burning television or a trouser press full of dynamite, but a new hearth or a brick dog kennel.

Moon's spiritual ancestor in this regard was John 'Mad Jack' Fuller, the eminent Sussex squire who peppered the landscape around his home with funny little buildings just because he could. In a field part-way along the Battle to Heathfield road you can still see the evidence of one of Jack's finest whims.

The Sugar Loaf, also known as Fuller's Point, is a conical stone structure, poking up from the edge of an empty field like the iceberg tip of a giant underground witch. It is named after the conical packets of sugar which used to grace grocery counters and was built, if you believe the legend – and it's too entertaining a legend to not believe – to win a bet.

Some time around 1820, Mad Jack, chatting with the vicar of St Giles' church in nearby Dallington, claimed that the Reverend's spire was visible from his home. When the vicar doubted him, the squire proposed a wager in the ever-popular 'I Can See Your House From Here' format. Fuller put his money where his mouth was, stomped home, threw open the shutters on his upstairs window to try and spot St Giles' steeple, and discovered there was a hill in the way. Before anything as dull as good sense could seize his mind, he rounded up a team of workmen and ordered them to build something that would peep above the trees and look like a church spire from his house. Bingo. Bet won.

Since all Fuller really required was a silhouette, it's good to discover that the Sugar Loaf has a door in the bottom and several fascia windows. It's fifteen feet in diameter, thirty-five feet tall and was lived in as a two-storey house until the 1930s, an example of how follies so often start off as a nice little idea, then spiral out of control surprisingly quickly.

Inside the folly is delightfully clean. Erected in a town centre, an eye-catching shelter like the Sugar Loaf would be full of urine, litter and twelve-year-old heroin addicts within minutes. Here, in the pretty Sussex countryside, the only sign of abuse to the structure are polite graffiti from courting couples through the years, names that ache of a lost age of hiding in follies for a snog: 'Cliff and Hazel, 1967'; 'Arch and

Ethel, Jan 1954'; 'Val and Fred, 6 June 1976'. With the setting sun peeping round its edge, the Sugar Loaf looks like a druidic monument, as satisfying and apparently purposeless to modern eyes as a dolmen.

The man behind this stupid structure is a fascinating figure. John Fuller was born in 1757, attended Eton, and served four times as a member of parliament. A massive, Falstaffian, John Bull character, his family fortune was propped up on the unpalatable pillars of war and slavery – as a cannon manufacturer and Jamaican sugar plantation owner. He was a High Tory of the old school, loudly opposing emancipation for both West Indian slaves and Roman Catholics in his strident, booming voice. In February 1810, he was thrown, drunk, out of the House of Commons by the Serjeant-at-Arms for rather too forcibly expressing his views, leading to a fight with the Speaker of the House.

In that classic obituarist's euphemism, Fuller 'never married'. As usual, those two words hint at a rich back story. It is said that Jack never recovered after his proposal of marriage was rejected by Miss Susannah Arabella Thrale in 1790.

Thrale sounds like quite a catch. Her crooked legs and umbilical rupture made her very short tempered, leading to her being nicknamed 'little crab' by her siblings (whether as a reference to her demeanor or her gait is unclear). Though her portrait shows her looking pretty enough in that gangly Regency debutante way, her father's pet name for her implied he thought she looked like an owl. Whatever Susannah's charms, Jack took the rebuff badly. A letter of the time by a family friend refers to his being 'so very angry with (Miss Thrale) that he has brought down a woman of the Town to Tunbridge Wells on purpose to distress her by following her everywhere.' Susannah, as might be expected under the circumstances, eventually ran off with a watercolourist.

Fuller used his fortune for a wide range of philanthropic works (none quite as philanthropic as the abolition of slavery, but there you go, these were different times). Notably, in 1829, he spent 3,000 guineas to save fourteenth-century Bodiam castle. Bodiam has a touch of the folly about it, which may have appealed to Fuller. It's not much of a practical defensive structure, more a vain display of ostentatious wealth by its original owner Sir Edward Dalyngrigge, making it one of the most satisfying pieces of idealised knights-in-armour architecture in the UK. It was, incredibly, scheduled for demolition before Fuller stepped in because its owners wanted to re-use the stone. Looking at Bodiam now, reflected romantically in its fairytale moat, this seems unthinkable, but proposals such as this were common in an age before our national livelihood depended on tourists queuing up to see the country's pretty bits. Even as recently as the 1960s, the Sugar Loaf itself was threatened with demolition. Thank goodness the locals stepped in and raised the £450 needed to save it.

Like Liverpool's Joseph Williamson (see the entry on the Williamson Tunnels), Fuller instigated many futile building projects (such as walling in his entire estate) to help alleviate unemployment amongst the poor. Fuller's other generous acts included shelling out £10,000 to help found the Royal Institution in London, establishing two still-extant professorships in chemistry and physiology, and becoming a sponsor to Michael Faraday. He also bought a barrel organ for Brightling Church (which survives as the largest working example in Britain),* put up a

---

* This wasn't Fuller's only contribution to the Brightling music scene. On hearing the noise made by the church choir, he subtly expressed his displeasure by buying and sending them nine bassoons.

wooden lighthouse at Beachy Head, and provided the first Eastbourne lifeboat. And between all these sensible and admirable projects, he found time to enliven the Sussex countryside with pointless stone nonsenses.

The Sugar Loaf is only one of Fuller's follies. The horizon line of his estate is enlivened by several delicious oddities. There is a Greek temple, an obelisk, a tower from which he may possibly have intended to watch restoration work on Bodiam or possibly just erected for the hell of it, and an observatory with a floor so wobbly that the telescope was practically useless.

Fuller was a patron of the artist Turner, whom he commissioned to immortalise his grounds and follies in paint. In one watercolour, entitled *Brightling Observatory*, Fuller's wobbly stargazing edifice is a tiny, pale block on the horizon, lost amongst the glorious swirls of cloud that obviously fascinated Turner much more than what he was actually meant to be painting. Only an artist as in love with the sky as Turner could manage to ignore the peculiar things Jack Fuller had chosen to build on the ground.

Mad Jack is buried, entirely appropriately, under

a twenty-foot pyramid in Thomas à Becket church, Brightling. His brooding, black mausoleum looms over the nearby houses like a newly landed alien spacecraft. Jack had planned well ahead, and the pyramid was standing for a full twenty-three years before he found a use for it by dying. So odd was Fuller's reputation that no-one batted an eyelid at tales of his having been buried seated at a banqueting table in a top hat, with a claret bottle within reach and the tomb floor covered in broken glass so the devil would cut his feet on entering. The tall tale turned out to be nothing more than that when, during restoration in 1983, the tomb was opened revealing nothing more outlandish accompanying Jack's journey into the afterlife than a few lines from Thomas Gray's 'Elegy Written in a Country Churchyard'.

Mad Jack is so much a part of East Sussex culture that he has given his name to a local pub in Oxley Green, and an image of his Sugar Loaf forms the official logo of Hastings' 'Mad Jack's Morris Dancers'. Very much a man of his age, his taste for fripperies has meant his memory has been preserved. He was even immortalised on a PG Tips tea card –

surely the highest honour that can be bestowed on any Briton.

These days, people with far too much in the bank tend to do admirable or comprehensible things with it, like giving large amounts to charity, or blowing it all on skiing holidays and sports cars. How much better would it be if they splashed the spare cash about on permanent architectural monuments to enchant future generations, like Mad Jack did?

Perhaps a system of favourable tax breaks for folly builders might encourage such behaviour. Sir Richard Branson could stop ballooning about like a ninny and get on with constructing a willowy free-standing steeple somewhere, and the national lot would be improved a hundredfold if Sir Elton John put some of his monthly flower budget towards building an underwater kingdom.

Fuller preferred his alternative nickname of 'Honest' John Fuller, which is hardly surprising, but it is for his eccentric use of his fortune, for the 'Mad Jack' side of his personality that he is best remembered. History is full of people who made lots of money, founded fine institutions and sponsored excellent artists. What there are too few of are people who spent time, wealth and effort erecting monuments as gloriously daft as the Sugar Loaf. They should be encouraged.

Keith and Dufftown Railway

I think the carrot infinitely more fascinating than the geranium. The carrot has mystery. Flowers are essentially tarts. Prostitutes for the bees.

Bruce Robinson, *Withnail & I*

Britain loves its trains. We might moan about actually having to travel on the things, but the idea of trains gets us all gooey and steams up our glasses. Guides for foreign visitors take great care to define the trainspotter as a British cultural archetype and, for generations, the default ambition for all sensible little boys was to be an engine driver.

Although the romance has been tarnished some-what by blandly branded private rail operators using computerised Tannoy voices to apologise* for the necessity of weekend bus replacement services due to permanent engineering works, insidiously slipping in the word 'customer' where 'passenger' would have better described their responsibilities to transport people rather than just take their money, plenty of us still harbour childhood dreams of running our own branch line, if only to see if we could do the job better.

In the sweeping wilds of Scotland a group of enthusiasts have managed to make their dreams come true, finding themselves an abandoned little two-stop line to run as their own, shuttling tourists to and from the distilleries of Dufftown through the dry-brushed scenery of Scotch Whisky country. And marvellously, they manage to deliver all the charm and nostalgia of old railway travel without ever resorting to anything as obvious as a steam train.

---

*Being apologised to by an electronic device, an idea which ruins the whole point of politeness by automating it, is surely the modern equivalent of the fantastic hat-tipping machines that W. Heath-Robinson used to draw.

The owners recommend that you start your journey in Dufftown, at the end with the marginally prettier trackside scenery, but it doesn't really matter which way round you make your trip. We started at Keith, just to be contrary, but there are only two stations, so you can't miss your connection or get lost. The ticket price is a no-nonsense £10 whether you're a grandmother or the Duke of Edinburgh. Nevertheless the elderly gent serving in the Keith station ticket office will painstakingly check the return fare in the relevant leaflet, taking his time in the way we all used to before some damn fool set the pace of modern life at 'too fast'.

The waiting room is decorated with authentic 1970s and 1980s InterCity posters, the first clue that, although this is a heritage railway, it is celebrating a more rarefied form of nostalgia than is exploited every time a locomotive puffs towards the camera through plumes of steam in a Sunday teatime telly serial. It's easy to wallow in the glories of the age of steam, but fewer and fewer of us actually lived through the thing – it's a borrowed affection from the previous generation. The memories stoked by the Keith to Dufftown line are of more recent vintage.

Waiting on the platform is a great opportunity to

observe men with pipes in their natural habitat. They are taking a chance to glimpse the future of retro rail travel. In a few decades, all nostalgic railways will have InterCity electrics haring along them, pandering to the memories of the sons and daughters of the men with pipes, who will whisper to their children that they remember when this was all electronic indicator boards. A beautiful thought. Apparently, an InterCity was spotted on the Keith and Dufftown line recently, but the organisers think it was probably just lost.

When it arrives, the train is one of two diesel electrics belonging to the enthusiasts who run the railway. Workhorses from the 1960s, these machines have a bluff, sturdy quality that is being superseded without you knowing it by the European slickness of modern rail travel. It is possible that you won't even have noticed how many trains have mimsy automatic doors that go 'pishhht' these days until you get on at Keith and realise that pulling the door shut was like closing a bank vault.

The carriages here are all outdated 'slamstock' – the railwayman's magnificent term for the mighty beasts whose doors thud shut at the platform guard's hand like a twenty-one gun salute before the train pulls out. Naturally, this glorious old sound of the railway is currently being phased out in the wider world thanks to yet more Tedious Health and Boring Safety legislation devised by mousy little twerps who weren't allowed to climb trees as children. If the owners want to get more young people to ride their railway, they could do worse than emblazon the word SLAMSTOCK in huge letters on their posters, so that kids think it's a skateboarding festival.

On board the train, it's Eastern Europe – austere, functional and forty years out of date. The signage (No Smoking, For God's Sake Don't Climb Out Of The Window, that sort of thing) is covered with the old British Rail logos that you don't see anywhere any more. Without them you might just think that you've got on a normal train on a normal quiet rural line. It's like finding an old credit card that never got thrown away, and suddenly appreciating the subtle differences in the graphics. You are watching nostalgia being born.

You could ride in the First Class section but only Standard Class tickets are available; Heritage railway enthusiasts wouldn't dream of infringing British Rail ticketing regulations. There isn't a Quiet Carriage on this train but there certainly is a bleeding cold one.

If you're planning a trip in the winter months, do take a pair of gloves and a fireplace. Either that or try and bag a seat at the warm end. This part of the train is soon pleasantly filled with lovely old ladies in cagoules all having a wonderful day out, and enjoying a complimentary snifter from the Buffet Car (included in your ticket price, which is more than you get in Standard Class anywhere else these days).

The Buffet Car is a proper guard's van with a trestle table. Thanks to their sterling work at fêtes and jumbles throughout the nation, trestle tables are of course the real backbone of Britain. One ought to be included on the Union Jack somewhere. It's good to see one going about its business here, groaning under soft drinks, wine and bottles of top-notch malt whisky (ask your steward for a recommendation – Glenfarclas is rather nice).

Don't forget to bring along your best flannel to keep the condensation off the windows. An important part of enjoying any day out in Britain is to sit behind some steamed up glass, probably with a pork pie and a flask of Bovril. There are almost certainly stretches of the year where the eleven miles of pretty scenery are unobscured by water vapour, but you can always breathe heavily on the windows to simulate a Proper British View.

At Dufftown, there's a welcoming little station and a chance to eat sandwiches in the rain, or grab a bite to eat in the stationary buffet car in the siding. The scale is small, low-key and friendly, helped by the comfortable familiarity of rolling stock from the day-before-yesterday. The ex-railwaymen and train hobbyists who have turned this abandoned branch line into their personal Hornby layout have got themselves a terrific toy. They can hopefully continue a tradition that would otherwise have died out, of taking tourists by this rail route to visit the world famous Glenfiddich distillery (which, it's good to report, remains a family owned business and smells fantastic).

For the average railway fan who has ever day-dreamed about owning a full-size train set, this is that dream come true. Without their beloved diesels, the people behind the Keith to Dufftown line would never have been able to get their project off the ground. These thrifty runabouts are cheap to purchase and ready to roll as soon as they're bought, needing little restoration.

Romantically puffing steam railways are now the

preserve of the Pete Watermans of the world – a millionaire's plaything. A new boiler for a steam train can cost upwards of £50,000, and their furnaces are constantly hungry for expensive coal. If a steam engine breaks down, it takes ages to fix, and for ever to fire up a spare locomotive to pick up the stranded passengers. Most vintage steam lines keep a diesel or two in reserve for when their star players are being temperamental. It's also worth saying that your pretty-looking antique carriage with its corridor down one side and its separate compartments is hopeless if you want to look out of the window. When they're not steamed up, the 1960s carriages of the Keith and Dufftown boast acres of unimpeded glass through which to admire the view, which is after all the point of this sort of day out.

This railway is a new attraction, and is unlikely to stay this way for ever. Appealing to family parties is essential to the line's survival, and the owners make no secret that they'd coin it in if they had a steam train to play with – bung a wizard on top of it and Voila! it's the Hogwarts Express. Draw a face on the front and pull in the Thomas The Tank Engine fans. It's a shame the Rev W. Awdry's railway stories tended to portray the diesel engines as the villains.

Had Daisy (the nice diesel) been a more popular character, the people here could have done a promotional deal, painted the front of one of their engines with eyelashes and put out some kid-friendly pamphlets – 'Come and meet Daisy, the Metropolitan Class Cammell 101/102 Diesel Mechanical Unit'. Don't you want to see a coin-operated one of those outside Asda?

In the meantime, until fashion catches up, the Keith and Dufftown line is a reasonable dream come enchantingly true. An attractive stretch of railway that would otherwise have fallen into disuse, saved by plucky, unglamorous rolling stock that will surely one day be as adored as the pampered steam divas we must all, frankly, be getting a bit sick of by now. Here's to Daisy. Her time will come.

EastEnders Set

Blessed is he who expects nothing, for he shall never be disappointed.

Alexander Pope letter to John Gay

Television and films are great for tourism. Fans love to make pilgrimages to places they've only ever seen in two dimensions, then take two-dimensional photographs of these places to bring home and show other people to prove, that, yes, it looks just like it did on the telly.

Cashing in on lengthy on-screen adverts for a pretty backdrop did no harm to the Yorkshire Dales

(*Last of The Summer Wine*), Castle Howard (*Brideshead Revisited*) or Ireland (any film with penny-whistles on the soundtrack that makes Americans go weak at the knees). This is the future of tourism – the location as media star. The locations don't even need to be real. Successful backlots where films and television programmes are made will throw their doors open, in emulation of the famous Universal Studios Tour in Los Angeles, and have fans queuing round the block. It's all part of the pizzazz and fizz of showbusiness, tapping into the broad, all-encompassing fame that the mass media can create.

Naturally, this sort of thing is totally against the spirit of this book. So, it's good to report that arguably the biggest, most popular, most talked-about British TV programme of the past few decades wants nothing to do with this sort of tacky cash-in. *EastEnders* not only has no interest in offering fan tours of its set, it actively wants you to bugger off and leave it alone. And because the only thing more British than someone wanting to be left alone to get on with their own business is someone else wanting to peek over their garden fence and see what they're up to, we reckon there's an Uncommonly British Day Out to be had here.

Filmed for the past twenty years in some secluded corner of Hertfordshire that is forever Walford, the BBC's flagship soap opera (unless you're a fan of *The Archers*) operates a closed door policy towards its always fluctuating army of followers. So if you want the British equivalent of a flashy studio tour, you'll just have to make one yourself.

Let us not leave you under any misapprehension here; this is never going to be the most rewarding day out. This is a spur of the moment outing for a sunny Sunday afternoon that would otherwise be filled with strimming a lawn, or not playing tennis, or watching the *EastEnders* omnibus. To get anything at all out of this excursion you'll be standing on tiptoe and squinting into the distance, attempting to spot the top of something vaguely familiar. These are minor thrills at the lower end of cheapness. Pack an exciting lunch (one with an unusual chutney, perhaps) and try and make your own fun. That's the spirit.

You're not going to be able to get anywhere near the set, and no one is about to condone any attempt to pole vault over the barbed wire. Security is dauntingly tight; there must be more cameras stopping the great unwashed getting in than there are filming the show itself. So ignore the gatehouse entrance at

Even grown adults can pretend to be goblins at
Blackgang Chine.

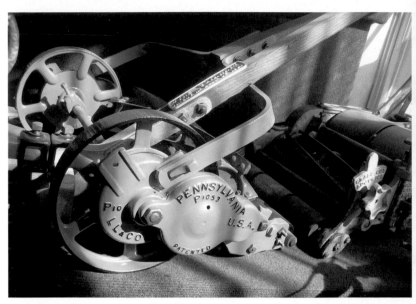

A pride of lawnmowers at dusk.

One man in a boat at Peasholm Park.

Sean Connery and Gorden Kaye, together again
at last, at Louis Tussaud's House of Wax.

Kelvedon Nuclear Bunker's famous
Telephone At The End Of The World.

We watched this four times.

Britain's pointiest pointless structure, courtesy of
Mad Jack Fuller.

Clickety-bonk, clickety-bonk, clickety-bonk.

The number 15 from Victoria Road to Walford town centre.

A witch in a bottle in a drawer in a cabinet in the dark in the
Pitt Rivers Museum.

A typical Cumbrian scene at
Eden Ostrich World.

Mixmaster Keith Harding's
Victorian wheels of steel.

A suburban taste of the Orient.

Beckham's glamorous beginnings.

A drop of the hard stuff. Mother Shipton's ruin.

the junction of Essex Road and Clarendon Roads, slip down towards the corner of Malden Road and start peering.

Look over the roofs of the new-build homes for your first sighting of Walford, E20.* From here in the somewhat less famous postcode of WD6, the railway bridge leading to Walford East station seems tantalisingly close. According to the version of the London Underground map used by the show's Cockney pretenders, Walford tube is on the District Line between Bow Road and West Ham. That's the position occupied by Bromley-by-Bow in the real world, which is why none of the characters ever say they're going to Bromley-by-Bow. The entire fabric of their world would collapse into a black hole if they ever did. Now that would brighten up a Tuesday evening.

From here you can see the tops of the house façades that make up George Street, E20. Because those BBC set dressers aren't stupid, you'll notice there's not a satellite dish in sight. Any character

---

*The actual postcodes in East London only go up to Woodford's E18. Neglecting the supposedly aesthetically displeasing E19, E20 was chosen for its roundness – surprising considering that it has a square at its heart.

living on this outlying street is usually on borrowed screen time (witness the latter days of Beppe di Marco and the brief sojourn of that bloke who used to be on *Blake's Seven*).* The heavy-hitters all 'live' in the centre, in the Square itself. And you're not going to get the merest sniff of it today or probably ever, without spending several years at a reasonable drama school and catching the eye of a casting director in a jolly mood, so heads down and walk up Malden Road. You may notice a sign or two attached to properties backing on to the lot reminding amateur paparazzi that these are private residences, which is fair enough.

These Borehamwooders can get a bit shirty when it comes to *EastEnders*. Letters to local papers complain of late-night filming and unruly teenage groupies hanging around at the entrance. This didn't happen when Flanagan and Allen or The Great Gonzo used to film here.† Despite this, property

---

*Oh, what was his name, again? Ah. Oh. No, we know this. Oh! Ted Hills. That was it.
†The Clarendon Road site was once a home from home for Crazy Gangs, Muppets and the boys from *Auf Wiedersehen, Pet* (whose original building site later became Albert Square). *Star Wars* and *Indiana Jones*, not forgetting *Digby – the Biggest Dog in the World*, were all filmed in another studio complex close

prices haven't been much affected one way or the other, according to one resident (who freely admits to taking advantage of his famous neighbours by chucking the occasional bag of rubbish over his wall for the BBC to dispose of).

A footpath now leads you from the end of Malden Road to Welbeck Close. At the end of a row of houses to your right, teasing you from over somebody's garden fence, is a bus stop marked 'Victoria Road (towards Walford).' The number 15, the number 657 and the N15 all stop here apparently. As with the tube, this is based on official London Transport routes through east London. You can stand here for hours and not see one bus turn up, just like in the real world.

Now stroll along Stratfield Road in the vague direction of a gigantic block of flats. Keeping the Elstree boundary to your immediate right, a peer through a wire fence a little further along the path reveals the entrance to Holby General hospital, previously assumed to have been at the other end of the

by; over the years six of these local studios have come under the catch-all of Elstree, the parish within which most of Bore-hamwood lies.

M4. This area also enjoyed a comprehensive career as the exterior of Grange Hill School for a few years in the immediate post-Tucker Jenkins era. BBC blackberries growing through a fence here look delicious during the late summer. You paid your licence fee, so in a sense you really ought to take some – £126.50 worth, or £42 worth if you want blackandwhiteberries.

Eldon Avenue takes you along the third side of the studios, turning right into a grubby access road that runs behind some shops for the fourth, before linking up with Clarendon Road once more. And that's pretty much it. The unofficial tour of one of Britain's modern cultural institutions.

There are many attractions you can go and see that are run by self-proclaimed eccentrics. Now it's your turn to behave oddly. This is a chance to spend some quality time looking at something you can't see. It's also a good way to celebrate an admirable and increasingly rare example of something enormously popular not being wrung for every last exploitable penny in the name of 'brand extension', or whatever they're calling it this week. If you want to make this little soap pilgrimage, the pleasures are going to be as small, sad, sweet and inexplicable as a four-hour trainspotting session on an abandoned branch line or a day by the riverbank catching no fish.

Be British, be strong, and be determined to enjoy yourself on a grand day out – no matter how futile it may be. Cue drums.

Pitt Rivers Museum

The world is so full of a number of things, I'm sure we should all be as happy as kings.

Robert Louis Stevenson,
'Happy Thought,' *A Child's Garden of Verses*

The University Museum of Natural History in Oxford feels, inside and outside, like a pocket version of London's Natural History Museum, which it predates by a good twenty years. It was amongst the favourite haunts of one of Oxford's most famous scholars, Charles Lutwidge Dodgson, known to the world and its daughters as Lewis Carroll, and appropriately the museum is full of reminders of his books. A stuffed white rabbit in one display case cradles a pocket watch, whilst a painting of a dodo by Flemish artist Jan Savery is almost certainly the basis for Tenniel's *Alice* illustration. Best of all, tucked away at the back of the museum behind a giant crab is a magical Wonderland-inspired arched double door with 'Pitt Rivers Collection' ornately inscribed above it on the frame.

Walking through the arch is like stepping inside Dodgson's mind – you find yourself in a dark, cluttered world of hand-labelled bottles, opium pipes and drawers full of bizarre looking keys, entered through a doorway apparently two or three sizes too small for the room it reveals.*

Lieutenant-General Augustus Henry Lane Fox Pitt Rivers (a name crammed as full as the man's cupboards must have been) began amassing interesting things in the mid nineteenth century. Starting with

---

*Although Pitt Rivers' hall of weird and wonderful objects looks as if it would have been the perfect trigger for Dodgson's rococo imagination, this awesome miscellany was first put on display here in 1884, nineteen years after the publication of the first edition of *Alice in Wonderland*, so life imitated art, rather than the other way round.

weapons and quickly moving on to everything else, he had soon gathered a pile of curiosities from all corners of the globe. Fascinated by Darwin's *Origin of Species*, he saw similar rules of evolution in the shaping of human artefacts – the way, for example, that primitive lumpy wooden padlocks seemingly made by trolls evolve effortlessly over the generations into elaborate, graceful keys that look like they've been designed by very clever swans. Pitt Rivers also wanted to show how different cultures have independently developed similar tools to resolve identical human problems. (We all need to keep our heads warm and dry, but look at all our different hats.) He even coined the term 'typology' to describe this classification by purpose.

Although that might sound approachable enough, the museum can initially seem pretty dark, fusty and bewildering. Many people's initial reaction to the mess of objects is confusion. Whatever you do, do not attempt to look for an eighteenth-century gallery or a cabinet full of objects specifically originating from the Polynesian Islands. It will prove impossible. Just keep in mind the magic word 'typology' and suddenly the whole experience opens up, ripe for browsing. Aha! Those distant islanders' quaint superstitions are filed in a cabinet next to your grand-mother's quaint superstitions. If it were here, your great-grandfather's crack pipe would sit in a case next to a more recent, smaller model from Hawaii. The Pitt Rivers Museum reminds us that all over the world, people are continually attempting to achieve the same things, and finding slightly different ways of going about it.

The next barrier to overcome is that it's so dark that you can't see anything at first. Signs apologise for this but explain that light levels are kept deliberately low to preserve the delicate exhibits. It can take a good twenty minutes before your eyes adjust, loris like, to the gloom. The helpful assistant on the front desk will happily grant permission to take photos, without explaining that most of them will come out as black rectangles. Keep some pennies aside for postcards.

The labelling of the artefacts is an exhibit in itself, and a good guide to when the object was added to the collection. Small, handwritten 'Drink Me' labels date back the furthest, followed by index cards, type-written notes and finally computer database print-outs. It is clear why successive curators have had to keep such scrupulous records of their growing haul of acquisitions. The museum's umbrella description is 'anthropological,' but that's really just an excuse to throw off all restraints and go collecting crazy. Anthropological means 'what people do,' which covers just about everything except clouds and squirrels.

It's hard to know where to begin. Four cabinets at the far end of the ground floor promise drug-taking paraphernalia. One is labelled 'snuff taking equipment,' one 'opium taking equipment' and two, yes two, cabinets are reserved for 'betel chewing equipment'. Betel leaves obviously require so much apparatus to enable one to chew them successfully that it's no wonder someone got fed up and invented Benson & Hedges. And the sheer weight of global superstition that filled the cabinet full of 'Charms Against The Evil Eye' can't help but start you worrying that you really ought to be carrying one yourself. After all, a lot of people have spent a lot of time making things to ward it off; it must be terribly important. What's the use of checking you've got your phone, keys and cash card every time you leave the house if you leave your enchanted string of sheep's ears behind and – bang! – the evil eye gets you?

This is the sort of museum that normally only

exists in films where bespectacled professors of Egyptology get their necks snapped by angry Mummies. The displays are so cluttered that the easiest way to respond is to give them a cursory once-over-and-wow as you walk past. But on closer inspection every cabinet turns out to be full of something fascinating: an assortment of ivory backscratchers; scale models of natives' huts; dozens of international thumb pianos – that sort of thing. You have to stop and pay proper attention to be able to piece together the connections between individual items, but it is hugely rewarding work.

Try not to be frightened by the sheer amount of information on offer. Pick a section and take your time, accepting that you'll never see it all. The collection sprawls over three floors, with every conceivable square inch of space covered with something unusual and interesting. Look up to the ceiling running round the first floor gallery and you'll notice that it's covered in hundreds of oars, nailed up there because there just isn't room anywhere else. You can picture Pitt Rivers returning home from a jaunt with yet another crateful of oars, putting his head in his hands and bursting into uncontrollable tears.

Finding your way round is part of the fun. A

brainwave from one of the curators in 2003 saw torches being handed out to children at the entrance, a spot-on idea which enables youngsters to illuminate the displays like detectives looking for clues. On busy days, the lancing beams turn the museum into a spooky attic full of weird and wonderful clutter.

And if it's spookiness you want, the museum delivers. A large case on the ground floor is draped with a purple velvet curtain, adding an unnerving M. R. James frisson to the act of uncovering its contents. By now you've seen so many grotesque and bizarre items that you wouldn't be surprised to discover the glass case contained a life-size Victorian wax effigy of you being fed to a giant stuffed wasp. In reality the curtain hides nothing more terrifying than some delicate Hawaiian feathered cloaks, but it makes you wonder why every museum doesn't cover its exhibits in bits of coloured cloth. It would make even the dustiest shelf of flint arrowheads appear frightening and secret.

It isn't just the cloaks that are hiding. Although it may sound incredible, the items on display at eye height are only the tip of the iceberg. There's a whole other museum going on at ankle level. Glass cases are often two-storey affairs; crouch down and discover a

whole new layer of shrunken heads or musical whist-
ling arrows. As if that weren't enough, some of the
display cabinets contain drawers, most of which can
be opened, like a dresser full of forgotten socks, to
reveal an overflow of further curiosities.

The top few levels of each cabinet, though full, are
glass topped and tidily labelled. Further down, on
the other hand, things get a bit messy – drawers
cascade with unorganised antiquities, the anthropological equivalent of a sideboard full of nameless
keys, broken souvenirs and foreign coins with holes
in them.

Sir David Attenborough, in his excellent introduc-
tion to the collection's guidebook, claims that Pitt
Rivers could be seen as one of Britain's earliest truly
interactive museums. Sure enough, there are a few
hands-on feely boxes stowed under the display cabinets, but these almost feel like a Johnny-come-lately
acknowledgement of modern curatorial trends.
Tugging out drawers is a far more exciting form of
interaction. It's refreshing that the collection doesn't
appear to have been edited in the slightest. Modern
museum styling often tends towards the minimalist
ideal: a big room with a single selected exhibit placed
on an award-winning pedestal with really nice

lighting. Visitors here, by contrast, are trusted to look at anything they want, whether it's on display or filed away.

It's certainly worth seeking out the drawer marked 'UK religious artefacts'. It contains the following labelled items: 'Two mole's forefeet carried in a small bag as cure for cramp (Sussex, 1911)'; 'Astragalus of sheep carried as a cure for rheumatism (Suffolk, 1911)'; and the star of the show, 'Tip of human tongue which was actually carried for a considerable time as a charm (Tunbridge Wells, Sussex 1897)'. The surprise of finding that these arcane charms originate from Britain is trumped by the realisation that they were donated as recently as the beginning of the twentieth century. We may think we have advanced in leaps and bounds since then, but don't forget we still haven't found a cure for the Barefoot Doctor.

Items like these keep the museum from becoming a Ripley's Believe It Or Not collection of colonial 'oddities'. To the curators of Pitt Rivers, whether an artefact originates in the affluent modern West or the dark jungles of the nineteenth century, we are all humans, and our junk is always worth studying. There may be a display of skulls and photographs from societies that practise head shaping and neck elongation, but they are placed alongside a single silicon breast implant (with the acidly written label 'surgery on a healthy person purely for appearance's sake first became popular in America in the 1920s').

That such a dark, old-fashioned looking museum should not only make us question our position in human civilisation, but also manage to be so popular with children with torches is testament to the scope, range and presentation of the collection. Its very old-fashionedness works in its favour, proving that there's more than one way to get people to interact with museum exhibits. Allowing visitors to discover whatever they want from the collection by simply leaving everything out to be picked through is the purest, cheapest and most invigorating type of inter- action of all. There are things that an overflowing Victorian chamber of delights can do that no amount of flashing screens and loud noises could improve. Sometimes all you need is a witch in a bottle in a drawer.

Eden Ostrich World

A hen is only an egg's way of making another egg.
Samuel Butler, *Life and Habit*

Plainly typed on a map or small brown roadsign, there are certain combinations of words that fire the imagination, and others that don't. For all you know, Molford Hall might be the most magical place on earth, with chocolate lakes and a giraffe rodeo, but you're not going to make a detour based on the name, so the sign zips past on the hard shoulder, ignored. Spot the words 'Eden Ostrich World', however, and you're cutting left across traffic, rescheduling your plans for the afternoon and excitedly jiggling about in your car seat like a five-year-old full of Sunny Delight.

Anyone with a rudimentary grasp of zoology will confirm that ostriches are the funniest animals on the planet. And when Eden Ostrich World opened in 1998, they confirmed this by inviting top TV funnybird Emu to peck through the tape. Freud can stick his theories on humour wherever he fancies – there's just something inherently comic about a bird as big as a person.

Anticipation of hilarious man-to-bird confrontation is high as you enter, paying a very reasonable 40p for a bag of rabbit dirts and sawdust, which is apparently ostrich mucsli for feeding time. You are also given a rock-festival wristband promising an access-all-areas afternoon in an emu moshpit and an evening watching the acts on the NME New Ducks Stage.

But the secret of comedy is, of course, timing, so you're not presented with the ostriches straight away. Langwathby Hall is a big, working farm, full of other delights, and there's plenty to see before you go head-to-beak with the stars of the show.

Langwathby specialises in odd variations of the

traditional picturebook farm animals. As well as chickens, you get ostriches, so by the same logic, as well as pigs, you get peccaries. Even a tiny horse isn't unusual enough, so their Shetland pony is a pony/zebra cross called Pozee.

The farm's valley setting is spectacular and practically silent. If you arrive at a quiet time it's so soothing it's almost eerie. It's a relief when a few school holiday parties arrive and start making kid noise.

And children are very well catered for. Little pedal tractors litter the farm like the please-take-one white bicycles of hippie Amsterdam. Kids can get on, ride, and abandon them whenever they like. It's good to see facilities handled like this, rather than doling out the tractors from a hire cabin to a hot, stroppy queue clutching £2.50 tokens.

The space between enclosures is peppered with unfussy, fun playground activities. As well as a see-through maze made of chicken wire (a good example of making use of what you've got), there are rope slides, tyre swings, a tiny Cresta Run on rails, go-karts: the sort of unsupervised playground equipment you thought was made illegal twenty years ago.

Best of all is a dangerous-looking combine harvester brooding rustily in a corner of the farmyard with tempting steps and ride-on appeal. 'Please supervise your children at all times' reads a legally cautious notice screwed to its side. Pah! This is just the sort of makeshift climbing frame on which decades of British children have grazed their knees. Who could begrudge the next generation the chance to learn from sharp experience?

In spring and summer, Langwathby's incubator sheds are filled with eggs the size of toddlers' heads, humming away. Eden's ostriches – African Blacks – can lay up to 100 of these in a year, the largest eggs of any living bird. It would take about forty minutes to boil one, if you were very hungry, and they require the biggest soldiers of any egg (half a farmhouse loaf should do it).

By now you're probably dying to fill some beaks with bird dinner, but be patient. Frankly, the eggs are unrewarding to feed and the pellets just slide disappointingly down the glass of their Kobi Big Bird egg-turning machine. In the next hut, however, are the ostrich chicks.

The chicks are billeted in the same enclosure as the ducklings and goslings, which makes the whole process even more fun. You're feeding a tiny ball of yellow mallard fluff when suddenly a doe-eyed, crew-cut thing the size of a small dog muscles in to get some nibbles. Ostrich chicks nip gently, but painlessly, and are enormously rewarding to play with. It helps that you can, for the moment, tower over them even if you're a child. In a minute, things will get more serious.

At the top of the farm are the adult ostrich enclosures. It may seem strange that such an exotic animal can be reared in the English climate, but ostriches are very hardy, and can be farmed in temperatures as diverse as Alaska's and Ecuador's. The male ostrich is the posh ballerina one from Disney's *Fantasia*. The females and youngsters are the brown, scruffy ones who look like Ken Dodd's head mounted on sticks. Ostriches would make excellent Christmas decorations.

The birds' enormous eyes and binocular vision mean they're constantly tilting their heads to focus on you. This is very appealing: after all, quizzical is cute. They seem fascinated and mystified by you, and it would take a hard heart not to find that flattering. Anthropomorphism is a dangerous thing, you tell yourself, but, dammit, these birds can't take their eyes off me . . .

African Black ostriches are extremely docile, but

their sheer size makes them intimidating dinner guests as they rifle through your bag of feed. There's another reason you might feel a little nervous. Because recent research suggests that birds are the direct descendants of dinosaurs, most modern movie monsters have borrowed their flocking and pecking behaviour from observations of flightless birds. Squint your eyes and you could be at a dinosaur sanctuary. The ostriches' squamous Tyrannosaur feet don't help matters much.

The chicks were easy, but the adult birds prove to be a whole different kettle of feathers. It is advisable to take care with cameras, spectacles, sunglasses and prominent parts of your face. You might start wishing you had something to feed them with apart from blunt, round pellets – something longer that would keep your hands well clear of their beaks. A Peperami, perhaps, or an orange on the end of a billiard cue.

What could be more exaggeratedly British than this high-octane version of feeding the ducks? Revel in it. Explore the edges of your fear. One of the most stressful experiences a human being can go through, next to bereavement, divorce and moving house while it's on fire, is facing an ostrich who's worked out that the food's coming from that little paper bag in your hand. It's all part of the game.

Disappointingly – and you may want to look away now to avoid having your illusions shattered – the ostriches refuse point blank to bury their heads in the sand. Apparently this is a myth which developed from sightings of the birds tending to their eggs, stored in shallow ditches. Another bit of knowledge learned from cartoons bites the dust.*

Of course, no trip to a working farm is complete without a potter round the farm shop, and this one's a cracker. You can get your own back on any ostriches who nipped you by buying their relatives in delicious steak form, or pick up a ready-blown ostrich egg as an unusual desk ornament. And there's always the ultimate kitchen-bookshelf conversation starter – a copy of *Cooking Ostrich With Confidence* by Sandra Hildreth, racked alongside *The Emu Farmer's Handbook*. This isn't just a good place for an afternoon saunter amongst some big, funny birds. It could change your career.

So, not just unusual and inherently comical, but educational. Plus a climb-on combine harvester to

---

*Unlike the ostriches.

boot. After years of foot-and-mouth gloom, it's nice to wander round a farm, even a tourist-attraction one, that feels positive, exciting and fun. Sometimes the promise of those little brown roadsigns is delivered in tractor loads.

Keith Harding's World of Mechanical Music

Life seems to go on without effort, when I am filled with music.

George Eliot, *The Mill on the Floss*

In the good old days, so they say, we used to make our own entertainment. We kept ourselves amused by sitting round the hearth telling stories, singing songs and hitting each other. Then along came television, radio, wind up gramophones and compact hi-fi systems and spoilt our fun. Or so they say. What rot. Some of our ancestors weren't having any fun at all. Think of the poor talentless people. Whereas nowadays, having no discernible party piece is a near-guarantee of 'celebrity' (since doing nothing whatso-ever minimises the chances of the public disliking what you do), imagine being a mediaeval mediocrity. Unable to play the lyre or dance a strathspey, you'd run out of things to fill the long winter evenings fairly sharply. Boredom might be the only option. May as well bugger off down the stocks and throw tomatoes at the weirdo.

Keith Harding's World of Mechanical Music is a sprawling, tinkling, ringing, crackling, chiming, piping, crashing and banging museum of home entertainment. It celebrates the history of the music machine – any device designed to take the tedium out of a night in for people too talentless or just too busy to bother to learn the sackbut.

The term 'mechanical music' is broad. After all, an iPod, a CD player or a doorbell is a machine that takes information from a source and turns it into music. Here, in the golden Cotswold village of Northleach (opposite the Dolls' House shop), are the ancestors of those musical devices we now take for granted, from clock to box, pianola to polyphon and gramophone to phonograph.

Keith Harding started dealing in antiques while still an engineering student. When he and partner Cliff Burnett began running a small business repairing musical boxes in 1961, they went in search of information about self-playing instruments, and found that there was very little available. Craftsmanship, like magic, has a habit of disappearing with its proponents – for example, at the time of writing, there are three people left in Britain who can build and repair globes. This statistic may not sound earth-shattering, but, you must admit, that it is in the true sense of the pun, bad news of global importance.

The principles of the music box are simple enough – a comb of tuned tines is plucked by pins that are usually arranged on a rotating cylinder powered by clockwork. You probably know the sort of thing: grandmothers' trinket boxes used invariably to have one, complete with lugubriously rotating ballerina. Harding and Burnett diligently learnt as they went along, developing techniques to build, tune and refine these music boxes. Pretty soon, with a lack of any real competition, they simply marched to the front of the mechanical music world and started claiming their prizes. In 1971, they published a book on music box repinning (stemming the tide of amateurs effecting repairs with nails and gramo-phone needles) and started producing good quality replacement combs.

In 1974, Harding delivered a paper, *The Ethics of Conservation*, to the British Horological Society, which is now an internationally accepted work of reference. Three years later, on Jubilee Day 1977, the one o'clock news featured Harding and Burnett's Silver Jubilee Polyphon, a replica nineteenth-century jukebox that played 20-inch discs. Their next big commission, a clock for an exhibition at the Victoria and Albert Museum with all its workings visible, started a trend for horological sculpture that saw many a shopping centre adorned with some sort of giant clock with its guts out.

To the visitor, though, perhaps the biggest surprise is that the Victorians had a jukebox at all. Long before the milk bar set had a whole scene going, daddy-o, their grand-daddios had a prototype Wurlitzer in the form of the coin-operated polyphon. This was a development of the music box, but with a simple twist: instead of the tines, bells or pipes being told what to play by pins mounted on a rotating cylinder, the data was conferred by a huge metal disc full of holes.

This is a striking discovery, because if you've ever seen a *How The Blazes Does That Work?* -style diagram of a CD, it's precisely the same thing: pits burned into a spinning disc. Indeed, there are many such modern analogues here. There's the piano roll, for instance. They crop up in cartoons – a long scroll of perforated paper that fits into a modified piano (called either a pianola or a player piano) which reproduces all the keystrokes that were recorded on the roll when the piece was played earlier by a qualified pianist. This is the direct forerunner of the modern MIDI file used in anything from a Pet Shop Boys album to a mobile phone ringtone.

Many notable names from the late nineteenth and early twentieth century left us piano rolls of themselves: Debussy, Ravel and Gershwin, for instance. Here in Northleach, you can actually hear George Gershwin playing a piano, live, in front of you. Or, for that matter, Grieg, Paderewski or Rachmaninov. Any of them will give you a private posthumous recital. It's eerily beautiful: the keys move under the touch of invisible fingers. You're standing at the shoulder of a ghost.

The museum, which looks like a cluttered Victorian parlour, is awash with antiquities that have modern descendants. There are horned gramophones, musical automata (including a lion tamer), barrel organs, wax cylinder players and carillons. But the real stars of the collection are the musical boxes, some of which are intimidatingly detailed. The pins on a musical box are eleven thousandths of an inch in diameter – that's a little over a quarter of a millimetre. They look like the trimmings from a brass man's beard.

Mind you, the pins are far from the smallest things at the World of Mechanical Music. Behind the scenes is the workshop, a haven of rare craftsmanship and seriously tiny odds and ends. Here drawers overflow with springs, screws, washers, keys, winders, endstones, barrels, balls, dyes, shellac and stopwork. One machine cleans surfaces by blasting them with 25 micron glass balls. Woe betide him who drops a bag of them.

Keith Harding insists that nothing leaves the workshop until it is as perfect as he and his colleagues can make it (and, by gum, he's thorough). In some cases, they have corrected mistakes made by the original manufacturers. Before attempting the restoration of a musical box which once belonged to the Sultan of Constantinople, Harding spent three months listening to Turkish music to get the vibe. Most satisfyingly of all, the Swiss – who, you might think, would be the crowned kings of mechanical music – now defer to Harding and Burnett's exacting restoration techniques. Yah boo cuckoo.

Perhaps surprisingly given the Luddite howling that comes from the music business any time someone introduces new technology these days, the advent of early mechanical music was wholeheartedly embraced by the musical community. Beethoven and Mozart both wrote pieces for musical clocks. Beethoven's contemporary, Haydn, wasn't going to allow his short deaf rival to get one up on him, so he rolled up his sleeves and turned out three dozen pieces for the things. In the last century, the wonderfully scatty American composer Conlon Nancarrow decided that pianists didn't have nearly enough fingers to play the number of notes he'd written as fast as he wanted, so he wrote pieces specifically for player-piano. Neat trick, but it spoiled the fun of a concert because there was nobody for the audience to applaud. If you've never heard of Nancarrow, this is why.

This is a house of rich history and pinpoint workmanship, but above all, it's a house of music, and a real pleasure – especially on the guided tour – to stop and listen. There is so much music in this little treasure trove that you sometimes hear snatches coming from other rooms, straining to get out and be heard – from a scratchy 78 rpm acetate of Harry Lauder to one of the collection's anachronistic one-offs, like the discs of Dave Brubeck's 1959 hit 'Take Five' made for the Victorian polyphon. Music is an ever more expensive commodity: a fiver these days will buy you a third of a CD or a thirtieth of a Glastonbury ticket, so a visit to Keith Harding's World of Mechanical Music is extraordinary value for money. Home entertainment certainly isn't spoiling Mr Harding's fun.

Shah Jahan Mosque

The early editions of the evening papers had startled London with enormous headlines: 'Remarkable Story From Woking'.

H. G. Wells, *The War of the Worlds*

The Surrey commuter belt. Leatherhead, Dorking, Esher, Godalming. It's just a case of unfortunate geography; these towns wouldn't sound half as funny if they were in Dunbartonshire. There's nothing actually wrong with any of them but for too long they've been comic bywords for middle England with all its negative connotations. Seventies sitcoms may never actually have been set in Godalming but the lead character's reactionary mother-in-law often lived there.

Woking is smack in the centre of this perceived Nimbyland, a haven of comfortable introversion where everyone is supposed to thrive on a diet of quietly suppressed suburban paranoia and its associated newspapers, shivering equally at scaremongering tales of murderers in the potting shed and cholesterol in the butter. Loyalist Woking proudly boasts a palace of which Henry VIII was rather fond. Delia Smith, the doyenne of the Surrey fondue set, was born in Woking. You can't get more Home Counties, more names-not-house-numbers, more can-I-put-you-and-your-lovely-wife-down-for-the-Rotary-Club-raffle than this. This is the Britain that writes stiff letters to the local paper when the pub on the green puts Thai food on the menu, saying it's all very well for the big cities but is it really what we need here? So it's a delightful surprise to discover that Woking is home to the nation's first purpose-built mosque, and it's been a part of the local community for more than a century.

With its charming courtyard rose garden and vibrant Metroland sunrise-motif gates, the Shah Jahan

Mosque looks every inch the traditional English place of worship. You won't hear a muezzin, it's all done quite discreetly here in Surrey; the call to prayer is remotely operated, setting off electronic devices in the surrounding subscribing suburban homes. The listed status bestowed on the mosque reflects not only its fine aesthetic qualities but also its important position within Britain's Islamic history.

It's thanks to the altruism of a Hungarian polyglot that this particular mosque is here at all. Born in Budapest in 1840, noted linguist Dr Gottlieb Wilhelm Leitner found himself working as a translator for the British army in the Crimea at the precociously young age of fifteen. By 1865 Leitner had achieved more than most of us can be bothered to in a lifetime; while already employed by King's College, London, as a professor in the Oriental department that he himself had established, he was appointed Principal of the Government College in Lahore, on the Indian subcontinent. Even that wasn't enough, so after improving the college to the extent that it was redesignated the University of the Punjab, he packed his solar topee and set off for the logical next stop for an expert in Oriental culture – Woking.

Now master of more than fifty languages, his continuing determination to persuade the cultures of the East and the West to shake hands led him to create an Oriental Institute in the town. Built during the 1880s on the site of the former Royal Dramatic College (which didn't exist for long enough to become a university, despite backing from blockbuster novelists Dickens and Thackcray), the Institute awarded degrees to its predominantly Asian students through its ties with the University of the Punjab.

Leitner well knew the importance of providing a mosque for the substantial Muslim contingent he had attracted to Surrey. With considerable financial assistance from Her Highness the Begum Shah Jahan – one of four consecutive female rulers of the Indian state of Bhopal – the Woking Mosque was finally completed in 1889. The glorious Mogul-style dome and minarets were no Brighton Pavilion-style pastiche, they deliberately echoed those of the Taj Mahal, built by the Begum's male namesake more than two centuries previously. In marked contrast to the Taj Mahal though, the Shah Jahan can only accommodate up to 50 worshippers at one time. This was epic Mogul architecture at a parish scale.

Mosques were not totally unknown in Britain at the time. Cardiff and Liverpool both had their own

already,* albeit converted from pre-existing buildings and thus less distinctive innovations for the
national roofline. Since the Suez Canal had first
opened for business in 1869, demand for seaworthy
Brits had outstripped supply; bringing many Muslim
sailors – known as 'lascars' – and dockworkers to
Britain to pass on their expertise. They naturally
needed somewhere to worship, so whatever was
available was pressed into service. Woking's mosque,
however, can claim the prestigious status of Britain's
(and possibly Western Europe's) first purpose-built
mosque.

The Oriental Institute could not and did not survive Leitner's death from pneumonia in 1899. There
was simply no one with the passion to carry on his
endeavours. His plans for a similar Hindu temple
and synagogue fizzled out when he did.

The institute didn't get demolished, but one-time
Woking resident H. G. Wells had a pretty good go at

*Liverpool's mosque – a modified terraced house – later
became the registry office where Ringo Starr married Maureen
Cox. Many religious temples have convoluted histories. The
Brick Lane mosque in the East End of London was previously
a Huguenot church, a Methodist chapel and a synagogue.

it in *The War of the Worlds*. Wells' narrator describes how 'the Oriental College burst into smoky red flame' at the end of a Martian heat ray, and notes in horror that 'the pinnacle of the mosque had vanished'. Displaying the best of Earthman pluck, the hero then enjoys afternoon tea with his wife even though bits of chimney are landing in his flowerbed. It is a mark of how much Leitner's exotic addition had become an established feature of the local community that, picking a recognisable landmark that the reader might be shocked to see vaporised, Wells plumps for the mosque.

Following his death, Leitner's family began to sell off the land surrounding the mosque. James Walker, a sealant company, moved in to the grounds of the former college and their Lion Works did sterling business here for years. When Walker scaled their operations down, the Mosque took over one of the disused buildings, which is now used for overspill for the ever-growing congregation at festivals and important times of worship, claiming the site back in a way that would doubtless have pleased Leitner.

Between 1899 and 1912 the Shah Jahan fell into disuse. With Muslim students no longer attending college in the area it lay forgotten, floors strewn with straw, until Leitner's son remembered it was there. He was in the middle of trying to offload the plot for a bit of ready cash when eminent lawyer Khwaja Kamal-ud-Din arrived to launch a successful legal challenge to the proposed sale. That's the thing with a mosque: it can't ever be owned as it belongs to Allah.

Khwaja established a Woking Mission with the mosque at its heart, and founded the monthly *Islamic Review*. For the next fifty years Woking and Kamal-ud-Din's mission were the focal point for Islamic Britain; scholars and dignitaries from all over the Islamic world would pop in whenever they visited Britain, and when the War Office wanted to counter claims that the bodies of Muslim soldiers killed during the First World War were not being treated in a manner befitting their religion, the place they chose to commission a burial ground was on nearby Horsell Common.*

Unlike the bigger and better-known Regent's Park Mosque, whose construction was permitted by George VI in return for a site for an Anglican

*Later moved to a devoted area in the Brookwood Military Cemetery.

cathedral in Cairo, the Shah Jahan Mosque came with no strings attached. It was built, not as a token tit-for-tat gesture, but because a visionary academic believed it ought to be. From the moment it was put up, it has been a public advertisement of the presence of the Muslim community in Britain, plumb in the heart of *Terry and June* country.

So, perhaps it's time for a break from the routine of visiting draughty old churches – if you've seen one reredos, you've seen them all. The Shah Jahan Mosque somehow combines the best elements of Indian Mogul architecture, British suburban style and rural parish church charm, and is outstanding evidence of a refreshingly longstanding tradition of British multiculturalism.

Beckham Trail

What is fame? An empty bubble.

James Grainger, *Solitude*

You may object on principle to the howling cult of celebrity that surrounds the likes of David Beckham, but Waltham Forest Borough Council's golden-balled celebration of their most famous son deserves an unreserved round of applause as an Uncommonly British Day Out.

It's a marvellous invention. Andrew Strickland, a particularly bright spark working for the communications department of the North London council, clearly woke up one morning in 2002 in a shining halo of inspiration. In the aftermath of the World Cup, sports fans from Torremolinos to Tokyo wanted a piece of Chingford's favourite son. So why not grab an *A to Z*, plot all the places David might have knocked a ball around while growing up, and publish it in the free council news sheet?

What turned a local interest story into a marketing triumph was the posting of the piece on the council website, under a catchy, Google-friendly name. Here it could be stumbled upon by David's eager devotees worldwide, many of whom might be looking to enliven their British holiday with an historically resonant day out. All Waltham Forest Council had to do now was to wait for the Japanese tourists to roll in, spending money in the region's cake shops and newsagents.*

The website notes that the trail 'has not been authorised, endorsed or licensed by David Beckham or any of his representatives'. Too right. This isn't part of the tacky tendency towards official £200 branded laces or signature socks that now blights the beautiful

---

*To this end, the council has translated the Beckham Trail website into Japanese and, more recently, Spanish.

game. This is the modern version of a canny Elizabethan innkeeper waiting for the royal coach to disappear over the horizon before nailing a wooden sign to the gatepost reading 'Queen Bess Slept Here'. It's opportunistic and cheeky, and in a fine British tradition.

To get the full spirit of pilgrimage, you may wish to attempt the trail on foot – thus using the same extremity that has gained David his fame. In which case, for the sake of saving some legwork, try missing out the first stop on the tour – Whipps Cross hospital, E11, where David was born – because it's miles away and looks just like a hospital.

Start instead at the Peter May Sports Centre on Wadham Road, E17, where David 'played for the under tens' side and scored more than 100 goals in three seasons.' This is located just off the North Circular Road in a pedestrian-unfriendly tangle of underpasses and scrubland that doesn't quite stretch to greenery, settling instead for tufts of disappointing brownery. There's quite a busy ants' nest by the Crooked Billet roundabout, and some white dog mess. Take a camera.

From here, the trail leads to Walthamstow Greyhound Stadium, 'where David worked as a £10 a night glass collector'. The unspoken rule of the trail, as will become clear, is that you don't ever go in anywhere or actually see anything. So stand outside and think about maybe coming back to do the trail with friends on a race evening (Tuesday, Thursday or Saturday), rearranging the order of stops so you end up here about seven-ish for a pint, a punt and a pie.

Further up Chingford Mount and taking a right onto Royston Avenue, you come to Ainslie Wood. David's grandparents lived in council flats near here, though the trail doesn't indicate which ones for reasons of privacy. So once again, there's nothing to see. Every few months, whenever Beckham pops back onto the news radar for playing football or combing his hair, television crews from as far afield as Brazil and Australia come to Walthamstow and follow the trail. Maybe they liven their reports up by having a kickabout between the trees.

The next stop is Chase Lane Junior School in York Road. David played for the school side, but he doesn't any more, so again there's nothing really to see. Hanging around by school gates these days will get you reported to the police, so move on quickly.

The trail then takes you to three separate parks

which David enjoyed as a small footballer. Larks-wood, Ridgeway and Mansfield Parks, like David's life, get increasingly posh. There's even a miniature railway and some rather pretty flower gardens. Strolling through Mansfield Park above the reservoir is extremely pleasant, the closest the trail comes to the sort of walk you'd do if it wasn't attached to a global sporting icon; the estates open up to reveal that peculiarly sunny, seasidey architecture that marks well-to-do London districts.

Through here, you come to David's very own Chingford Secondary School in Nevin Drive, E4. On the way, you pass the very fire station where, you almost expect the tour instructions to inform you, David would have worked had he decided to become a fireman. Standing outside this fire station is, to be honest, as exciting as standing outside Chingford School, with less risk of turning up on some sort of register or being mocked by teenagers. Take your pick.

Checking the map you have printed out from the website, you are now faced with a choice. The next location is an absolute age away. You've walked about ten miles by now and, according to the backs of your legs, the last stop might as well be in Scotland. But if you can make the extra distance up Daws Hill for a mile or so, you'll come to the jewel in the crown of the Beckham Trail – Gilwell Park. It is here, the guide tells us, revealing the depths of its genius, that 'David went on cub camp.'*

Time to turn towards Chingford instead and go to the pub.

You quickly suspect that the trail may well have been plotted out by picking all the areas in the region that are mown regularly and joining them to David's schools with a marker pen. But somehow, that's part of the charm. The main attraction has gone, to Manchester and Spain and fame as Britain's most enormous global footballing celebrity. You are following the ghost of something interesting, and it left ages ago.

An unexpected bonus is that, if you grew up somewhere a bit like this, the Beckham Trail evokes a strange nostalgia for boring childhood walks. Strolling for hours through housing estates is something

---

*This genius was recognised by the Chartered Institute of Public Relations, who presented Strickland's team with their 2004 Excellence Award in the heartwarming category of 'PR on a Shoestring'.

only small children who can't drive somewhere more interesting will do with their day. There's an overgrown back alley near the cemetery after Ainslie Wood, and picking through the weeds and chain link fences is gorgeously evocative of short-trousered days covered in nettle rash and sticky drink.

The trail is a wonderful and pointless Odyssey round somewhere so unremarkable, it would take the association of the most heavily promoted sports star in British history to make it worth a mention. But that very ordinariness means that if you wander between all these Council rec pitches and school car parks, using the back alleys and hidden footpaths behind the concrete pavements, stopping maybe to have a kickabout in a couple of the parks, then, yes, this is exactly what it would have been like to be the young David Beckham – because it's exactly what it was like to be the young anybody.

Mother Shipton's Cave and Dripping Well

The wisest prophets make sure of the event first.
Horace Walpole, letter to Thomas Walpole

Knaresborough doesn't really need a tourist attraction. Built on a gorge above the River Nidd, it's one of those places that would look fantastic on an overcast, pissy day from underneath an inside-out, torn umbrella, waiting for a delayed bus on the wrong side of the road. Quaint houses clamber up the steep, tree-lined hillside, the old cotton mill (now luxury waterside apartments, naturally) looks out over the rushing weir and for a moment the entire world seems to stop and congratulate you on having made the right choice for a-place-to-stop-and-take-things-in.

Whilst countless British towns would happily trade their grey, municipal, concrete back teeth for such a picturesque, chocolate box vista, Knaresborough seems to have it all and more. The lucky buggers have got a castle and a spectacular viaduct and a market selling quality local produce and an annual bed race through the river. And if that were not enough, to clinch it all, they have also got an historic petrifying well and the cave where prophetess Mother Shipton was supposedly born. And they're both in exactly the same place.

The cave and surrounding parkland have pulled in visitors for centuries, and the petrifying well, like many natural springs, has always been popular. People frequently came to bathe in its 'healing' waters, although they were probably in and out like a school shower for fear of solidifying.

In 1630, local rector Sir Charles Slingsby purchased from Charles I the land on which the well and Shipton's cave stood. Realising that he was now sitting on three or four potential money-spinners, he started to market the attraction more widely. Word quickly got round and soon crowds were travelling across England to visit the magical 'dropping' well and Shipton's eerie birthplace, and Slingsby was doing rather well. Clever chap, Slingsby, but cheeky: buying a natural phenomenon that belonged to the nation then 'reopening' it to the public was a bit like erecting a fence round a square of someone else's lawn and charging them an admission fee to come in and marvel at their own grass. Still, by exploiting what was there and landscaping some glorious woodland trails to cater for the Georgian love of recreational promenading, he created an attraction that continues to draw punters today.

Knaresborough's petrifying well is England's oldest paying visitor attraction. Before the invention of the steam generator, when the dodgem and the chair-o-plane were but distant rumbles in the future, this is what we did for a fun day out. And because it's a natural exhibit, apart from the recorded voiceover, a visit to the well today is much the same as it would have been in the seventeenth century. In an age before advertising, MTV and espresso had withered the national attention span, people came here in droves to hang an object from the 'dropping' well and watch, for ages and ages and ages, while it gradually turned to stone.

As with a lot of traditional magic tricks, science has made a humdrum school experiment out of what once might have seemed a miracle. But petrification has for a long time exerted a powerful hold on the human imagination; think of the myths surrounding the standing stones of Long Meg and Her Daughters in Cumbria, Perseus avoiding Medusa's deadly gaze, or Han Solo's carbonite tribute to the Morecambe and Wise dance in *Return of the Jedi*. The fossilisation of objects, now easily explained, can still exert a bizarre fascination; the enduring creepiness of the preserved remains of ancient Pompeiians being a good example, chilling us with the creepy rock-hard evidence of what nature can do when it gets cross.

If you prefer the magical world of mythology and don't want to know how the well turns things into stone, look away now (or like Perseus, view the following paragraph in a mirrored bronze shield gifted to you by the goddess Athena). The high mineral content of the water flowing over the rock face, over a period of months, gives the items hung in its flow progressive coatings of calcium carbonate, creating a rock-like crust. Eventually items are absorbed into the stone surface over which they were hung. For example, the two nostril-shaped formations on the face of the dropping well are in fact a top hat and Victorian bonnet, dangling here since 1850 and never collected. Countless items have been left for petrification over the years, and a selection of good ones, rescued before they turned into nostrils, are on display in a little museum.

For a start, you've got to take a look at Queen Mary's shoe, left after a royal visit in 1923, and now preserved like a granite gravy boat. Quite how she made it home after her kind donation isn't explained. Then there's John Wayne's hat. No, not that one. His favourite straw hat. And of course, as the jolly taped commentary by the well reveals, 'No exhibition of petrified items would be complete without something from famous magician Paul Daniels and Debbie McGee.' Naturally. And just in case you were wondering, it's McGee's toy rabbit wearing Daniels' bow tie. Now, that's not really magic. Especially considering that before selling off his shares and disappearing, Paul Daniels was joint owner of the Mother Shipton complex.

There is something curious about the idea of famous people leaving objects for petrification and not returning to collect them later. Is it some brazen display of wealth, that they can donate their shoes, hats and teddy bears without even caring? Certainly, there still appears to be a steady stream of notables queuing up to have random keepsakes preserved in stone for us ordinary people to marvel at. Celebrities from *Emmerdale*, *Coronation Street* and *Blue Peter* have left items for petrification (Bet Lynch's camisole, anyone?). Perhaps they get some warmth from the knowledge that these items will be on display in a Knaresborough museum long after their own careers are stone dead.

More watery fun can be had round the back, for up some steps is a wishing well. A sign gives very clear instructions on how to make your wish; place your right hand in the water, let it dry naturally, don't reveal your wish to anybody, don't wish directly for money or for harm to come to anyone. Apparently no visit to a traditional wishing well is complete without receiving a two-inch bruise on the crown of your head from standing up too quickly. Maybe you could wish for that not to happen.

Mother Shipton's cave on the opposite side of the path is a good place to soothe away aching heads and dry not-to-be-wiped hands. Bar the odd theatrical lightning effect, it's quite a peaceful spot where you can listen to the story of the woman born Ursula Sonthcil. At the back of the cave is a model of what looks like the prophetess herself after a few months under the petrifying well, predictably gnarled and twisted, and really just there to give your children nightmares for a good few weeks afterwards.

As the hook-nosed logo for the complex, poor Ursula can't help but come across as she has done for centuries of tourist exploitation: as a long-fingernailed supercrone, prophesying everything from the collapse of Knaresborough's first viaduct to the result of the 2.15 at Chepstow. You've got to wonder at how much of her tale is true, since most of it was taken from word-of-mouth accounts. Her prophecies were only set down in print in 1641; that is, suspiciously soon after Slingsby had opened his attraction to the public. She still pulls in the punters though, cheerily unaffected by her prediction (reported nervously in our vintage 1970s AA guide-book) that the world would end in 1981.

Depending on which entrance you take to the wells and cave, the museum either opens or ends your journey. Stuffed with petrified items, local history and photographs, it provides a useful bookend for the trip. As promised on the sign outside, a life-size waxwork Mother Shipton greets the visitor, with figures of three further local characters tucked away at the back of the museum – John Metcalfe, aka Blind Jack (famous road builder), Sir Charles Slingsby (famous drownee) and Eugene Aram (famous murderer). Aram hangs in his iron gibbet being constantly pecked to death by a crow, accompanied by an unnerving fifteen-second tape loop of hoarse cawing and groans of 'help me': an awful punishment for this celebrated villain, and also perhaps for the assistant working the shop till in front of it.

It's all part of one of the country's longest-running tourist packages though. Telling these tales in a slightly melodramatic manner preserves their magic. If Mother Shipton had not been portrayed as such a caricature, then perhaps none of her prophecies would have been remembered. If the 'magic' petrifying well had been sussed three centuries ago as nothing more than spectacular kettle fur, perhaps it would not have proved quite the same draw for tourists and passing TV magicians.

Even though we may not swallow the backstory any more, the reason people continue to visit Mother Shipton's Cave and the Dripping Well is fundamentally unchanged. It's a beautiful walk, in a beautiful part of the country with a folklore-filled grotto or two chucked in for good measure remaining, to this day, a most efficacious promenade suitable for the betterment of all known ills.

Apollo Pavilion

By a curious confusion, many modern critics have passed from the proposition that a masterpiece may be unpopular to the other proposition that unless it is unpopular it cannot be a masterpiece.

G. K. Chesterton, 'On Detective Novels,'
Generally Speaking

This is a story of good intentions gone dreadfully awry. It is the story of the British public's difficult relationship with modern art. And it is the story of a bold vision becoming the victim of its own ambition.

The Apollo Pavilion in Peterlee was, until the Angel Of The North spread her magnificent wings, the biggest piece of public sculpture in the North East. It was an audacious attempt to build a spiritual icon within a new landscape. It was beautiful, grand, and brilliant. These days, most of the locals will tell you it's crap. The truth sits somewhere between the two.

Peterlee (named after Peter Lee, a former miner, checkweighman, Methodist preacher, chairman of Durham County Council and clearly very busy man) was one of Britain's twenty-eight New Towns, built in a spirit of post-war optimism and the belief that good civic design fostered social harmony (they didn't know what was coming). Spanking new homes with radical roofs and prefabricated timber infill panels were built for 30,000 miners, around a well appointed, double-decked town centre.

In 1955, seeking an artistic mentor for the project, the Peterlee Development Corporation asked Victor Pasmore, then Master at King's College, Newcastle, to take over as design consultant for the development.

Pasmore's predecessor, Berthold Lubetkin, had just had two years of hard work rejected and, unsurprisingly, walked off in a huff. Lubetkin is probably best known for his work designing the penguin pool at London Zoo, which was so award-winning and Grade I listed that it ruined the poor birds' feet and they moved out. He went on to become a pig farmer.

Pasmore, one of the great abstract artists of the twentieth century, immediately seized the opportunity and created a piece of sculpture which he hoped would form an artistic focal point for the town. His design, named The Apollo Pavilion in honour of the NASA moon missions, was built between 1963 and 1970 at a cost of £33,000. A brave, handsome, superbly proportioned work of art, it ought to leave you boggling in awe at its striking design. In fact, as you scrape your chin from the Peterlee pavement, you are more likely to ask yourself whose stupid idea it was to put that there.

The Pavilion measures eighty-two feet in width and twenty-one feet in height, and is squeezed like a badly parked bus between the houses. The scale of the piece is completely disproportionate to its surroundings. It's as if somebody erected an oil rig in a suburban front garden.

The Pavilion is also in a miserable condition. The Peterlee Development Corporation used to look after the sculpture, in the days when it had fitted lighting and benches around it; the days when wardens regularly patrolled it and people ate sandwiches from greaseproof paper in its shadow. That idyll came to an end with the dissolution of the New Town Corporations in 1988, when Apollo came under the aegis of the district council, who could ill afford its maintenance. These days, it is an advertisement for nearly two decades of neglect: light fittings ripped out, panels rusted and wrecked, nails exposed, concrete spalled and heavily graffitied. Pasmore's two biomorphic murals have long since disappeared, as have a mounted plaque and the steps at either end of the platform. When photographed for this book, it had recently been cleaned and painted. No, honestly.

If it were an underpass or a multi-storey car park built in the same style, it wouldn't be any prettier, but the locals would look past it, satisfied that it was modern, not really their thing, but doing a job, earning its keep – that it had a function. Meant to just be beautiful, it fails because no-one round here really thinks it is, so they mistreat it and let it fester.

The steps that made the pavilion a usable bridge were removed by the District Council to stop local youths treating it as a climbing frame. So these days, anyone determined to clamber on top to enjoy ten Rothmans and some electric blue fizzy stuff will steal someone's wheelie bin or rip down a panel of their Waney Lap fencing to use as a bunk-up. In a further low-effort concession to their duty of care, the Council planted shrubs on the pavilion, hoping to beautify it. Sadly, they just make it look like a shoebox full of dead houseplants your neighbour promised to water while you were on holiday.

'An architecture and sculpture of purely abstract form through which to walk, in which to linger and on which to play,' was how Pasmore described the sculpture known colloquially as 'the Pivvy.' 'A free and anonymous monument which, because of its independence, can lift the activity and psychology of an urban housing community on to a universal plane.'

He was so nearly spot on. It is purely abstract, but only because you can't use it as a bridge any more; its freedom and anonymity have led to vulnerability and disregard; people do linger and play on it, but they leave their empties in the lake; and, most successfully, it *has* lifted the community on to a universal plane – of contempt.

It's impossible to underestimate the level of the

pavilion's unpopularity. The long-standing row about its fate has been wonderfully camp. One councillor insisted that it be blown up, and even invited the Territorial Army to supply the explosives. Pasmore suggested the army would be better off taking out the houses on either side. English Heritage chimed in, saying 'there's nothing like it in the country, perhaps not in Europe either,' and proposed that it be listed at the highest designation, Grade II. Tony Banks, then Secretary of State, refused the initiative because of the pavilion's reputation as a rendezvous for 'undesirable activities,' which is a bit like refusing to clean your teeth because they're already dirty.

Pasmore was clearly not a man to stop poking the hornets' nest once the fun had started. 'It's not designed for the present local residents, it's designed for future residents, so I would expect the present local residents to dislike it,' he added, blithely sailing past the logic that future residents are the ones currently smashing its lightbulbs and drinking cider off the top of it. He also insisted that the graffiti covering it 'humanised and improved it more than I could ever have done,' which is an admirable attitude for an artist. One wonders if Michelangelo would have been so understanding had somebody drawn a felt pen cock on the Sistine Chapel ceiling.

For all that, this 'hated 1960s sculpture . . . in a pool of stagnant water' as the *Northern Echo* charitably described it, is still worth a visit. It needs to be seen because it says something about the British public's relationship with art. Its story is a highly-strung version of the debate usually had in newspaper columns around the time of the Turner Prize, here played out in actual physical space with real people's lives. Like Lubetkin's penguin pool, it has charm and artistic merit, but is fatally flawed. Although the penguin pool is more popular because, as science will doubtless one day prove, humans prefer round things to square things.

Paying a visit to the pavilion is a faintly nerve-racking experience, even from the bespoke viewing platform. Children play in the drain, as though picking through the rubble of a blitzed city. They make toys out of debris. Teenagers linger, with no facilities locally and nowhere to go. Adults politely ignore the pavilion, as they would a recalcitrant neighbour. And there it glowers – too bloody close to everything, looming over locals and peering through their windows like a furious giant who wants to talk to you a bit too intensely about art.

The obvious solution would be to move the thing, lock, stock and reinstated stairways, to a big, flattering space, such as the grounds of a college or a kept square, where it might breathe and achieve the level of appreciation it deserves. Instead, at the time of writing, a £300,000 grant from the National Lottery is being sought to repair the pavilion and rescape the land around it to make it inaccessible to undesirables, and, disappointingly, everyone else. Shame, since that's the same solution that's ruined Stonehenge – that other great huddle of British grey slabs.

In its current position and condition, Apollo is Miss Havisham's cake, decaying defiantly in full view of embarrassed eyes. But, with a bit of luck and some public goodwill, perhaps the pavilion, like its classical namesake, will one day be regarded as an ideal of beauty and inspiration. In the meantime it stands as a marvellous monument to how stroppy the British can get when you leave art in their gardens.

Hamilton Toy Collection

And then I saw above me my old Corgi Toys Porsche Carrera 6 ... As I opened the box, I glimpsed the blue plastic engine cover first and felt a rush which transported me back to a summer holiday in Cornwall in 1967. And I was nine years old again.

Julian Cope, *Repossessed*

It's like finding out that Father Christmas doesn't really exist. Waking up on the morning of your tenth birthday expecting a Batman costume only to discover that your parents have chosen to give you a book token and a sensible pair of bicycle clips instead.

Toys, they insist, are for kids, and it's time for you to start growing up. This is humbug, pure and simple. Just ask the Hamiltons, the living embodiment of the old maxim that the family that plays together stays together.

Toy museums often have a slightly frosty presentation style: blank-faced display cases offering a handful of aged playthings alongside yellowing information cards. There's a sense of repressed fun about them, of a jack-in-the-box screwed tightly shut. School parties wander round, unimpressed by dour-looking exhibits that once thrilled children when glimpsed in the frivolity pages of the 1845 equivalent of the Argos catalogue. If this was all that Victorian kids had to play with, no wonder they didn't mind being sent up chimneys. It was probably the most fun they'd ever had.

Eschewing this tried and time to-be-rested approach, the Hamilton Toy Collection sprawls energetically all over its current home, a converted Perthshire guesthouse, as if a toybox had just been upended in preparation for playtime. If there's a square inch of display space left unused in any of the bustling rooms (which there isn't) then the owners have got a willing Matchbox Volkswagen Beetle or a

Fireman Smurf ready to fill it. At every turn something surprising yet comforting catches the eye, provoking an involuntary 'I always wanted one of them!' or an 'I had that!'

Each member of the Hamilton family is custodian of his or her chosen field, with separate rooms of the house given over to themed portions of the collection – mum's dolls, dad's soldiers, Hamilton junior's cars and so on. Any photograph in the displays of a child playing with one of the toys will likely be of one of the family themselves. This gives the museum a homely feel in keeping with its subject.

Philip Hamilton can remember early warning signs of his obsession surfacing at the close of the Second World War, when he swapped some strawberries with a friend for a set of lead animals. He seems to have got more long-term satisfaction out of the deal, unless his childhood acquaintance has opened a Rotting Fruit Collection we haven't heard about. Philip later developed a passion for model cars, then for Patsy who passionately married him. Luckily, Patsy wasn't averse to hanging on to a few teddy bears herself.

By the time their children Cris and Catriona were born the family already had access to a larger toy box than is probably sensible. Cris inherited his father's love of vehicles and is now in charge of the museum's hoard of electric cars and trains and Thunderbirds 2. If it has wheels or wings, he wants it, talking reverently of his collection of Raleigh Choppers – how excited he was at the announcement of the new limited edition bike for 2004; his five MkII versions in various colours; his search for that elusive 1977 Silver Jubilee model . . .

The family spent every spare moment at boot fairs and rummage sales, digging up treasures to satisfy their hunger. Young Catriona anthropomorphised in a fashion that would have made Johnny Morris's heart pound, buying the unwanted soft toys strewn over Sunday trestle tables because she felt so sorry for them. Having diversified into Games & TV Tie-ins, she later married novice collector John (Sci-Fi & Cartoon Figures) and they are now proud parents of the very young Callum, who has already been instilled with a love of Thomas the Tank Engine and Bagpuss in preparation for his inevitable inheritance.

There is so much here that the family constantly forget what they have and what's on display. There's no churlish pecking order to the exhibits based on monetary value or collector's cachet. At one point during our visit, Cris bubbles over with enthusiasm, eager to show off a rarer-than-gold James Bond Goldfinger Scalextric, of which only a handful exist in the world. Then he realises it's at the back of the TV room, buried under piles of *Magic Roundabout* jigsaws and *Charlie's Angels* action figures and can't be seen at all. 'It's in there, somewhere,' he says, satisfied that, should a visitor press their nose against the glass for a couple of hours, they might glimpse a corner of it, and that would be enough.

Homemade make-and-do classics also get a look in – we have no right to forget the humble knitted Clanger. Many kids would have owned a hand-built *Blue Peter* squeezy bottle version of Tracy Island alongside their mass-produced Power Ranger toys, so the Hamiltons celebrate it all. Even the once ubiquitous golliwog is present in book, doll and badge form, stubbornly refusing to be airbrushed from history no matter how unpalatable it may seem today. This is British children's history with all the lumps and bumps left in.

The Hamiltons only managed to open a permanent home for the exhibition in 1995, when Philip's retirement meant he no longer had to spend all day administering hospitals. Realising that the museum's visitors might not have quite the same taste in toys as they did, the Hamiltons grudgingly began to acquire items of which they weren't so fond, concentrating particularly on more modern items dating from after their own childhoods. Their haul is now representative of so many decades of British growing-up that it seems worthy of national collection status. All of the displays are reorganised and revitalised during the closed season, the cabinets tipped out on to the carpet to be sifted through. It's easy to picture the scene as Patsy sits on the floor, ministering to her eagle-eyed Action Men and button-eyed bears, trying her best not to play with them.

Across the landing from the doll quarters, her husband tends to his troops. Philip loves his soldiers unconditionally – metal or plastic, he shows no favouritism. His specialist room also contains cowboys, dashing knights on horseback and vintage sportsmen given away with packets of Sugar Puffs. Soldiers from different eras make tours of duty together. Boer War figures made during the actual Boer War cheer on the 1945 VE Day parade just a few shelves away, undisturbed by a nearby Coronation procession. Genres and epochs mix and melt. There are even figures from a child's lead gardening set

('You could eat a crocus soon as look at it,' says Philip) who seem quite happy to have been repainted as footballers and resold, complete with strangely crinkly legs where their shorts have been painted over long gardening slacks.

These tiny fusiliers striking familiar poses will tickle the memories of grown men who wistfully recall kneeling over improvised mud forts, fighting epic imaginary battles with the aid of rusty nails and the devastatingly effective Swan Vesta. It's a lost art. Toy soldiers are no longer produced in great quantities. Those that are manufactured keep to the old designs, with both eyes firmly on the collectors' market.

Nostalgia is a fragile thing, and its genuine form is getting rarer by the day. Blame the internet for making everything too accessible. Now that everyone can be reminded within a matter of seconds of the names of the *Trumpton* firemen and the precise measurements of a lime Spangle, it's getting harder to find anything that produces that misty-eyed feeling – the pull at the heartstrings brought on by something forgotten but once-familiar. Auction sites such as eBay should take the rap for allowing us to reclaim our entire childhood, plus the bits of everyone else's that we always felt denied, reinventing our toy cupboards in a shape they never really had, adult pocket money filling the yawning gaps in the Smurf collection. And let's not get started on that joyless practice of purchasing toys never to be released from their original packaging.

We throw out our old *Beano* annuals, safe in the knowledge that they can be repurchased for peanuts when more loft storage space is available. In the cavalcade of easy memories, we might rightly feel nostalgic about the very concept of nostalgia. Do you remember when we used to be able to enjoy 'Do you remember . . . ?' conversations in the pub?

The Hamilton Toy Collection helps to preserve our sense of nostalgia without taking it for granted. It isn't accessed at the click of a mouse button; we actually have to travel in order to be rewarded by its contents. Despite spending a whole afternoon there, the mind predictably proves incapable of holding on to the fine details of everything it has just tried to take in. But that's as it should be. Childhood memories require an occasional refresher course, not a televised twenty-four-hour drip feed of stand-up comedians pretending to remember how long it used to take to melt a Ninja Turtle figure in mum's wok.

The Hamilton family should, of course, be offered immunity from any charges of wallowing in Britain's cultural history. Not dour collectors or traders in false memories, but real enthusiasts, they have built a very big toy cupboard for all of us. They have surrounded themselves with their (and our) playful past for the common good. And then they have poured it all over their house. This is the loft of dreams. Go and have a poke around.

Imber

But there were no things there; there was nothing to show that this was a place where people lived, just bare steps, bare paint-peeled doors, hinge-pins sticking out of cracked gate-posts to show where there might once have been wrought-iron gates.

Oliver Postgate, *Seeing Things*

It happens all the time: you lend a book or rucksack or tenner to someone, and you never see the damn thing again. They start to get slippery about what happened to it, never quite coming clean that they've lost or sold or swallowed it. Eventually it's the first thing that springs to mind every time you hear their name. No matter how many rounds they buy or birthday cards they send, their name will forever be burned into the back of your skull as The Person Who's Still Got My Bloody Thing.

If that Bloody Thing was your home or, even worse, your home and all your neighbours' homes, and everything between and around them, the odds are that it would take some kind of grandstanding miracle to cheer you up. And miracles, as any cynic will tell you, don't happen. Just like they didn't at Imber.

On 1 November 1943, the army called the 135 or so residents of this tiny hamlet to a meeting in the village school room and told them that they had forty-seven days to gather all their possessions and leave. There had been speculation that this worst-case scenario might come about: the village, after all, was in the middle of the largest military training ground in the country, during the biggest war it had ever fought. Hundreds of British, American and Canadian troops had been stationed on Salisbury Plain, and there was a good chance that some unsuspecting civilian would end up getting a long-range gun test round the back of the head.

Over the next seven weeks, the people of Imber gradually left to find new homes and jobs. Some found neither, and stayed with relatives or wound up in workhouses. Farmers got rid of their equipment and stock, with more than 5,000 animals being sold on. Not a penny was paid in compensation for all of this, excepting removal costs and (in a spasm of extreme military generosity) a payment covering the value of any vegetables left behind in residents' gardens. The Baptist Chapel had a farewell service at which the congregation sang 'There Is A Fountain Filled With Blood'. Last orders (literally) were called at The Bell Inn.

Though they had mixed feelings, the villagers gladly did their bit for the war. The huge multi-national force gathering on the Plain was preparing for the invasion of Europe. If D-Day worked, the war could be over in six months. War Department officials told villagers they would be back at home before the next harvest. Cleverly, they told them to their faces, and forgot to tell them in writing.

Since this book is not called *Testikeln zu Altonschloss*, we can conclude that the Imber training exercises worked; the invasion of Europe succeeded, and the Nazi menace was defeated. But once the VE

Day balloons had been taken down and the final remaining celebratory spam sandwich had been scraped into the bin, the government and the military went a bit quiet. In the hush of peacetime, it was possible for the people of Imber to hear the sound of goalposts moving.

The village itself had, according to the original deal, not been intended for target practice, but the handful of people who sneaked back in found it strafed, blasted and potholed. Even the chapel and St Giles' Church, fenced off and signposted as consecrated ground, had been ransacked. And the whole place was crawling with alarmingly big rabbits.

Then, in 1948, the War Department let slip to *The Times* that because 'the Imber area as a whole is absolutely vital for training purposes, the decision not to allow the former inhabitants to go back had to be taken.' This was the first public confirmation that Imber had been permanently silenced.

That silence is still striking today. What remains of Imber (a fraction of what was there in 1943 when the military moved in) is a ghostly place. For most of the month of August, the army stops playing soldiers here and the village is opened to the public. The roads from nearby Heytesbury and Warminster are unblockaded, and St Giles' Church is unlocked. But even the highest summer sun has trouble flattering the place, which is a corpse of its former self. The windowless remains of Seagram's farm resemble a brick skull. The Bell pub is largely sealed up – even though, utterly improbably, its sign still groans back and forth on its hinges in the wind.

Stranger still is the lack of those little features an inhabited village would have if it had been allowed to survive into the modern era: roadmarkings, flowers, lamp-posts, litter, a phone code. There's no sign saying 'Welcome to Imber: twinned with Pripyat.' Instead, there are severe red notices reading 'Imber Village: Access Restrictions,' ordaining day and night speed limits for tracked and wheeled vehicles, and bald statements that anyone who fancies straying from the roads and hardstandings risks losing a limb to unexploded ordnance.

It's a cruel irony that the MoD added the word 'Village' to the boundary signs, because it isn't one any longer. Most of what was Imber has long been demolished to make way for standardised military training obstacles. Instead of cottages and barns, there are rows of dead-windowed breeze-block shells called Chester Flats – those grey boxes that look like they were designed in black crayon by a sad-faced five-year-old whose wicked stepmother locks them in the loft. You'd think the army would have had more sense than to requisition an entire village as a realistic setting for their war games, then raze most of the distinctive bits of it to the ground. They had thousands of acres of the Plain at their disposal; they could have built an unconvincing square-edged mock village anywhere. In fact, they did anyway, about three miles up the road.

The evisceration of Imber can't help but make you wonder what would have happened had it been left to thrive like its Wiltshire neighbours. There'd be the traditional split between the people from the ex-local authority housing at one end of the village and That Lot from the Posh End. The pub would have had a makeover, fancying itself as some kind of gastro-experience because it does burgers with relish rather than ketchup. There'd be the usual cast of village types: the minor celebrity, the spindly piano teacher in a tiny car, the tired and emotional *roué*, the pipe-smoker with a topiary fetish and a deafening wife, the retired fascist who frightens the children, the unconvincing cousins, twenty women called Penny, the bluff publican who definitely killed someone once, the weekends-only Stock Exchange tosser whose garage is full of wine and skiing equipment, the Oxbridge cobweb, the family with four caravans, the self-sufficient vegans with the pet alpaca and the redoubtable Man Who Keeps Asking You If You Want To Be A Bellringer.

But Imber isn't alive today. It's still on the map, although the dotted lines that used to be its approach roads make it look as if it's dissolving, fading into Salisbury Plain. Wandering round the village on an August afternoon is a solemn and faintly surreal experience. You don't have to be shown round: you can simply pick your own way through its dead lanes. Graffiti abound, and though there's no sign of a Wilfred Owen amongst the squaddies ('40 Commando are shit,' 'Wingnut Warrior,' 'Jock fucks' etc.) the walls scream with demands from the revolutionary-sounding IFF for the dead village to be returned to its owners, many of whom are now dead themselves.

It's not a bag of laughs, admittedly, but if you keep your eyes open there's plenty of black wit to be found, if sometimes Black Watch black wit. The saloon bar chalk board that would normally advertise Today's Specials is busy with military scribble, all arrowheads and flanking formations. One of the main arteries into the village – no doubt once a Deadmans Lane or Mockbeggar Ride – is now American Road. Imber Court, the most palatial home in the village, has a corrugated metal roof.

There are so few remnants of Imber's peaceful past still standing that those which survive are particularly precious. The seventeenth-century bell-rounds, notated in hand-wrought brick red script, are still visible on the tower wall of St Giles' Church. The bells are gone (removed, like so many others, for the war effort, though strangely we never saw any bronze battleships clanging out of dry dock in return), but there's no shortage of pealing during August thanks to a generator in the graveyard and a tape deck wired to a couple of speakers. It's primitive, but effective.

As you leave Imber, the glorious scenery along the roads is littered with the hulks of dead tanks. This is England's green and pleasant land, battle-scarred and brutalised. An uncanny Jerusalem. Like the village, it reeks of neglect. Broken promises, broken hardware – broken tombstones, even. The dead didn't get any peace here – or many visitors. Relatives had to apply in writing to the military for permission to pay their respects at family graves. Walk softly by the crumpled tanks. This is as close in Britain as you will come to No Man's Land.

Cumberland Pencil Museum

The pen is my terror, the pencil my shame.

William Blake, *To Thomas Butts*

There's no messing about at the Cumberland Pencil Museum. Within two minutes of arriving you'll find yourself clutching an excellent navy blue pencil topped off with a smart pink rubber. You didn't ask for it – it was a free gift when you paid the admission charge – but they're clearly trying to convert you to the joys of graphite and cedar wood before you've even stepped inside.

Designed as a showcase for the Cumberland Pencil

Company Ltd, it should come as no surprise that this good-humoured museum operates with single-minded missionary verve. It clings to the side of the factory in Keswick where Cumberland pencils have been manufactured since 1832, rolling off the production line in all grades from 9Hard to 9Black. The company used to make an F-Grade too, but it was discontinued so long ago that they can no longer remember what the F stood for.

The museum is full of little titbits like that. For example, it's reassuring to discover, as you stand chewing the end of your free pencil and reading the display board, that the good old Royal Institute of Public Health and Hygiene certified Cumberland Pencils as non-toxic in 1960. That's handy. Though it might be nice to get some Kendal Mint Cake to take the taste of paint and graphite away.

The entrance to the museum is a narrow passage-way through a plastic reproduction of the Seathwaite Fell mine in nearby Borrowdale. A disembodied yet somehow reassuring voice booms history at you from the ceiling, informing you that pure graphite was first dug up in Seathwaite in the early 1500s – the earliest recorded discovery of the substance in the world. Before someone worked out you could use it to draw nude ladies and bowls of fruit, there were several early unsuccessful experiments to burn it like the coal that it initially seemed to resemble. Soon, however, it was being exported to meet the demand of Europe's leading artists, a trade that soon led to a booming pencil industry here in the Lake District. It gives a warm sense of continuity with the past to know that Michelangelo would have written his shopping lists with an early version of the complimentary Cumberland pencil you have behind your ear.

For several centuries Borrowdale remained the world's primary source of the mineral which generations of Keswick natives knew variously as black cawke, wad, or the misleadingly vivid plumbago. The artistic demands of the world's scribblers were such, however, that by the Victorian era, Seathwaite's supply of graphite was all but exhausted. The company now makes its traditional Derwent range of products using graphite imported from China, Korea and Sri Lanka, but still under the proud Cumberland brand.

From the replica mine, the visitor emerges into a room that is simply groaning with pencils. If there's anything about pencil manufacture you're still not clear on by the time this museum has finished with you, then you really haven't been paying full attention. It's all covered: the billeting, the sieving, the extrusion, not to forget the ever-popular edge-runner milling. You can see the things at the raw, dipped, or grooving stages. Pencils don't just happen on their own, you know.

There are kids everywhere. It stands to reason that kids love pencils; they tend to use them, at home and in the classroom, far more than most adults. In the words of one of the schoolchildren who was present when we visited the museum, 'these pencils are great!'. For them, exploring the museum is part of a healthy fascination with the story behind everyday objects – all that stuff that boring grown-ups just pay for and take for granted.

See young eyes light up as they learn that one Californian Incense Cedar tree can provide enough wood to make 150,000 pencils. Watch them point excited fingers at the long, coiled green pencil lead, writhing in its display case like a bowl of wrestling worms. And there is a fairy-tale moral to the story that money-no-object NASA scientists spent millions of earth dollars developing the world's first zero gravity space pen, only for the thrifty Russian cosmonauts to launch themselves happily into orbit with pockets full of pencils.

A huge display tracks the evolution of Cumberland's pride and joy. Exhibits range from the pencil-shaped pencil of the days of yore to today's, well . . . pencil-shaped pencil. All properly obsessive museums share this trait: case after case of tiny, fascinating variations on the same thing. Even the design and graphics on the side of the pencils barely date. You could write with a 1940s pencil and no one would stare at you (unless they spotted that you were using the one with the Winston Churchill speech printed along the side). The pencil is a bona fide design classic, immune to the vagaries of fashion.

For those parents still suffering pangs of nostalgia for *Play School* there is a through-the-arched-window video presentation taking a look at the pencil factory in operation. Watching a machine churning out 600 perfect pencils per minute whilst another sharpens 400 in the same amount of time has a truly hypnotic effect. Andy Warhol would have been proud to have made this film, although he probably would have made it last for eight hours rather than ten minutes and there would have been more drag queens in it. The video loop ends with a clip of that enduring

Christmas favourite, *The Snowman*, drawn using Cumberland's finest pencils and surely the uncontested pinnacle of coloured pencil art.

By now you won't be surprised to learn that the world's longest pencil is housed here – it's 25ft 11in long with a yellow lead. It would probably seem a mite churlish for anyone other than a pencil museum to hold this record. If you're looking to take on a similar challenge, perhaps it might be more polite to settle for making a pencil just six feet long with an orange lead instead. It would be far easier to do and you'd still have the world's longest orange pencil.

But there's more. For the unconverted still moping round the exhibits muttering that it's all just a load of boring old pencils, the museum has yet another trick up its sleeve. Bring on the heroic undercover pencil. Originally envisioned by Charles Fraser-Smith, procurer of special equipment for the war effort (and the inspiration for gadget guru Q in Ian Fleming's Bond novels), this pencil was issued to POWs and Bomber Command aircrew during WWII. A Keswick-based team sworn to absolute secrecy carefully filled each of these hollow pencils with a tightly rolled map of Germany and a tiny compass. If this doesn't flip your wig, then how about the stunning sculpture of Bassenthwaite Lake made entirely from South African diamonds? (Oh all right then, it's made from pencils. But it's still stunning.)

Before you leave, don't forget to stop and chat with the delightfully charming and funny ladies running the shop. They seem happy in an almost evangelical way. Perhaps it's all that Kendal Mint Cake they're pushing from baskets on the counter. A diet of heart-racing translucent peppermint sugar and you'd be singing hosannahs to graphite.

The Cumberland Pencil Museum is a member of that fantastic breed of attractions that somehow manages to hold the attention by riffing over and over on the same narrow theme, until you just give in with a grin. All hail the pencil, sturdy workhorse of art and design. Come on, you've always wanted to know how one works.

Pack O'Cards Inn

'If I had all the money I'd spent on drink,' observed Henry, 'I'd spend it on drink.'

Vivian Stanshall, *Fall Of Felt Hats*

Once upon a time, a man won a game of cards. And though he was very pleased because he had won a lot of money, he wondered what to do with his newfound riches. And the man thought, people build temples to their gods, and monuments to their heroes, so I'm going to build something in honour of Lady Luck. And so the man built a big house in the shape of a pack of cards. And one day the house turned into a pub . . .

We British love our eccentrics, and there was one on the loose in Combe Martin in the seventeenth century in the shape of George Ley, local councillor, teacher, overseer of the poor and clearly all-round good egg. Faced with what was clearly a rollover-week-sized pile of cash, he knew exactly what to do to say thank you to the fifty-two cards, thirteen face values and four suits that had earned him his windfall.

On a plot of land measuring fifty-two feet by fifty-two feet, he built a four-storey house with thirteen fireplaces, thirteen doors on each floor, fifty-two stairs and thirty-six windows (the total of numbered cards in a pack). Now, that's what you call attention to detail. As to the shape of the building, it's perhaps best described as Very Hard To Describe. Yes, it does look a bit like a house of cards, but in common with a cash register, a motorcycle display team, Jimmy Savile's hairdo or the arrow hidden in the FedEx logo, it's a shape better seen than explained.

Admittedly, it does look increasingly like a pack o'cards the more pints o' beer you enjoy there. By 1822, Ley's folly was no longer a private house, and had started serving ales and letting rooms to coachmen and their charges for the night. It's still doing that today, as a lively and friendly pub with an impressively appointed games room.

Little is known of George Ley, which is a shame, because, if his silly monument is anything to go by, you get the impression he might have been the sort of cove who'd go fishing disguised as a tree* or walk from Land's End to John O'Groats in his pyjamas.† Today his name is mainly associated with an educational charity and this batty boozer.

It wasn't officially named the Pack O'Cards until June 1933, although everyone had been calling it that for years. A 1930 *Daily Sketch* advertisement for the then unremarkable sounding King's Arms Hotel made it explicit. 'Ye Olde Packe o' Cardes,' it said, '10 Minutes' Stroll from the Sea. Famous Ancient Hostelry. Teeming with historical features.' (The Pack O'Cards has certainly got a better claim to eccentric olde worlde appeal than a lot of pubs, whose catalogue-ordered Victorian clutter disguises the fact that all the original charm was torn out by

*Like Thomas Birch (1705–1766).
†Like John Slater (1947–), who now lives in a cave.

Formica-happy developers in 1976 to make room for more illuminated Watneys signs.)

The inn has always been a big attraction for visitors to Combe Martin, a cosy village on a particularly crunchy bit of the Devon coast between Exmoor National Park and Ilfracombe. The place's other claim to fame is that the road that runs through the middle of it is the longest main street in any British village (at nearly two miles). This sounds like a C-list world record at best, but you've got to admire Combe Martin's pluck: they capitalised on it by holding the country's longest ever street party here in 2002.

Like the inn, the village is one of those places that is a wee bit other, at a slight angle to the rest of us. For a long time nobody was in charge, since unlike the surrounding villages, Combe Martin had no squire, and it remains unashamedly different to this day. There's an annual hobby-horse event known as Hunting The Earl Of Rone, when the entire village hunts the errant Earl from Friday night until Monday morning, when he is found in Lady's Wood and thrown into the sea.

This ancient tradition has taken place in the village every year since 2000, when it was revived. (See, they like to do things differently here.) It had been off the annual fixtures list since 1837, when it was banned by a rector rendered blue with anger at the 'licence and drunkenness' of a three-day pub crawl that climaxed with a masked man wearing a string of ship's biscuits being made to ride back-to-front on a donkey. He even burnt the costumes, the big spoilsport.

But despite the best efforts of the authorities to stop them being silly, the people of Combe Martin still knew how to have a good time. In 1987, the entire village was humbled, amazed and plunged into darkness by *The Paul Daniels Magic Show*, which rolled into town in order to perform an enormous card trick. For a few minutes that night, The Pack O'Cards was a TV star as a gigantic five of diamonds two storeys high rose from its roof. The high street was closed off and electricity supplies interrupted.

There are photographs of this historic night in the Pack's modest museum, one of Britain's only such establishments that doubles as a skittle alley. The collection, like the building itself, is in need of some care and attention. Daniels' magical assistant, the lovely Debbie M'Gee (a very legal rendering of her maiden name on the picture caption) is slipping in her photo frame. A few pieces here and there have been stolen.

The exhibits tell the story of a building that, ironically for a monument to Lady Luck, has had its fair share of ill fortune. Two years before its TV appearance, the inn went into receivership. It was neglected and things started to collapse. It must be difficult enough to maintain as it is – to get to the top roof but one, you'd have to either clamber from a footbridge onto one big roof and two small roofs, or get onto the roof of the extension at the back, then climb the two roofs of the other extension, then shin over the two small roofs. Unless Spiderman's looking for a pub to manage when he retires, bits of it are always going to need a lick of paint.

The Pack got its first financial kicking from the Hearth Tax. At two shillings per fireplace, this was pricey for a building which had been built with thirteen of them as a joke, so Ley foxed the taxman by having the fireplaces feed into only eight visible chimneys (assessors would calculate the levy from the street). But when William Pitt introduced the Window Tax in 1696, things really hit the fan.

The bricked-up windows are visible scars the Pack wears to this day. It's a shame to think that such a delightfully odd building can have struggled so badly for survival, but perhaps that's why there aren't that many similarly crazy undertakings. There is, of course, the Grand Hotel in Scarborough, which is a sort of brick calendar. Built by Cuthbert Brodrick, it has 365 rooms, fifty-two chimneys, twelve floors and four turrets (one for each season). It's also in the shape of a V in honour of Queen Victoria. Her degree of amusement at this homage has gone sadly unrecorded.

The Pack O'Cards has had many eminent endorsements. Michael Parkinson honeymooned there in August 1959. His wedding night was interrupted by a policeman from Doncaster throwing a coal scuttle into the room in the early hours of the morning and flash-photographing newly married Michael and Mary as they shot up in bed. It would seem he suspected the couple were having an affair. 'Must have done too many divorce cases,' was the startled groom's charitable conclusion.

The inn is also home to a rare architectural feature, the bee bole. For the unfamiliar (that'll be all of us, then), this is an eighteen-inch square or round-headed alcove cut into a wall. Each bole would house a bee skep – a woven straw basket in which a hive can be established (see the chapter on Porteath Bee Centre). Bee boles are usually found in threes and fours on south facing walls. The Pack O'Cards, unable to do anything by half, has two stacked rows of six boles – presumably representing dice in a game of craps or somesuch excuse – all beeless at the time of writing.

The Pack O'Cards is one man's fragile fantasy, big and impractical, confounding and uncompromising, great fun and probably a blinding headache to look after. That's exactly why it deserves your attention. As our high streets, shopping centres, housing estates and theme pubs get more and more practical, sensible and convenient, at the expense of all looking exactly the same, we need tourist attractions like The Pack O'Cards so that Britain's towns and villages can tell each other apart. A grotesque pub in the shape of an indoor game, built by a lunatic and completely impossible to keep running efficiently is a fantastic reason to travel, because it's a fair bet you haven't got one of those at home.

Down the road from The Pack, Combe Martin is trying out a newer selling point: a high-tech dinosaur and wildlife park, where you can see dinosaurs in voguish animatronic form as seen almost everywhere

The Apollo Pavilion had been recently cleaned. Honestly.

Scotland's busiest toy cupboard at the Hamilton Collection.

Playing soldiers in the shadow of Imber.

Imagine the size of the sharpener.

The Ace of Pubs.

All the fun of the building site at Diggerland.

The tempting entrance to Lab 1 at Orford.

If you are a child visiting Exhibition Road, this is the cabinet that will give you nightmares for the rest of your life.

Tebay presents the ultimate truckers' cheeseboard.

A Williamson Tunnel within a Williamson Tunnel.

The unmistakeable atmosphere of
Barometer World.

Portmeirion – the quintessential Welsh Italian village.

Edinburgh Camera Obscura. It's just a trick of the light.

else from California to Kensington. So if it's a toss-up between a pleasant lunch in a mad pub or a face-to-face encounter with a pneumatic dilophosaurus, you are referred to the title of this book.

Diggerland

*Sirs, I have tested your machine. It adds a new terror
to life and makes death a long-felt want.*

Sir Herbert Beerbohm Tree

When Hugh Edleanu's plant-hire firm had an
open day to show off their diggers, dumpers,
loaders and excavators, he couldn't help but notice
that the children were queuing up to clamber all over
them. Perhaps Bob The Builder's friend Scoop was
to blame. Perhaps decades of Tonka and Lego were
the reason. Perhaps it was the basic thrill that many
a child knows can be got from sitting on dad's lap

'driving' the car. Whatever the explanation, Edleanu spotted an opportunity, and turned it into Diggerland.

On paper, Diggerland sets off all sorts of alarms in the head: lots of very powerful industrial machinery being operated by excited kids – it's the sort of vision from which Health and Safety officers wake screaming in the middle of the night. Anything that upsets such busybodies is obviously to be encouraged, and anyway, as soon as your five-year-old is at the controls of a JCB earthmover, it seems the most natural thing in the world. Anyway, according to the staff, accidents here are as rare as a pink digger.

It goes without saying that the first thing you see at Diggerland is yellow. So is the next thing, and the thing after that. It doesn't really matter what the things are, they will invariably be yellow. It's a whole fairground the colour of fresh egg yolk.

Like many theme parks, you buy tokens on entry, and spend them as you choose. Your choices here are all variations on familiar favourites; some taken from the funfair, most taken from the more old-fashioned village fête. You can play skittles from the cab of a tracked mini excavator, knocking the pins down with a lead ball suspended from its arm. You can have a crack at hooking an iron duck with the big pirate's-earring hoop attached to your JCB. You won't win a goldfish or a homemade Bakewell tart, because neither of those things is a digger, but apart from the prizes, it's surprisingly close to the sort of simple Fun Day that takes place on trestle tables on school fields up and down the country most spring and summer Saturdays. The spiritual ancestor of Diggerland is probably the local fire station open day, where children are allowed to have a go on the hose.

Though most of Diggerland's attractions proceed at the refreshingly clunky and un-theme-park pace demanded by heavy plant machinery, there are a couple of token concessions to the peculiar modern hunger for sickening centrifugal force. There's Spindizzy, a £118,000 tracked digger which holds eight people in its modified scoop and lifts them into the air while whirling madly round. (The member of staff operating it looks like he's having the time of his life.) And if you'd rather go up than round and round, there's the SkyShuttle, a £62,000 telescopic loader that shoots six people into the air. The price tags of the machinery aren't included here as proof of diligent research, or the result of a fetish with the cost of industrial equipment: Diggerland has them up on signs. It's handy to have the facts at your fingertips – for instance the giant diggers (JCB 8060s, in case you were wondering) cost four tokens to play on, or £38,000 if you want to take one home. Bring your chequebook.

Perhaps the main difference between big, modern theme parks and the small, old-fashioned village fête is that the park is a passive experience, where you sit still and are thrown round alongside everyone else, while the fête is an active one, where every toss of the hoop rings a different goldfish. Diggerland has a foot in both camps. You can be active in lucky dipping or racing round in a pedal digger, or be passively driven round the site in a digger train – a dumper-truck Surrey Without A Fringe On Top.

At one corner of the Strood site, there's an enormous snow machine, inactive when we visited, implying some kind of crazy diggerboarding activity might go on here. Nothing would surprise you, though: everything here seems to be the result of endless brainstorming sessions that all began with someone banging the table and saying, 'Gentlemen, I will not accept no for an answer. There must be something else we can do with diggers'.

It's difficult to imagine a theme park on a less glamorous subject, so it might be difficult to imagine enjoying a day out there. But, when we asked for suggestions for this book, Diggerland cropped up probably more times than any other. That's because it is a simple, slightly unhinged idea carried out splendidly. And because it has caught the public imagination: there are now three of them across the country, a fourth proposed for Castleford in West Yorkshire, and one in Dubai. What's more, because Diggerland is mostly big versions of small things (village fête games blown up big) rather than small versions of big things (the Disneyland-on-the-cheap problem that blights most British theme parks) it's intrinsically charming. Of course, there's a mascot, Metal Micky – but, crucially, he's just a logo on the brochure. They haven't forced anyone to shed their dignity by dressing as a seven-foot cuddly digger. The staff are a helpful (and bright yellow) bunch, savvy enough to know how the diggers work, should one of the dads ask.

After having as much fun as you can conceivably have in a digger, you'll probably want a bite to eat at The Dig Inn. (Applause.) And then, after a refreshing tumble on the bouncy castle (because children do things in whatever order will make them sick first), comes the encore: the gift shop. This is where the yellowness goes rocketing off the scale, and you begin to sense that Edleanu is on to something. Diggers, it turns out, have a serious young following. JCB has its own kids' club. And the toys, the toys . . . if you buy a JCB jigsaw here, it's not a cut-up photograph of something yellow, it's a toy saw. Diggerland even has its own brand of clothing – Diggerwear – so be prepared to go home with a pair of yellow wellies.

It is encouraging to think that a play park could inspire future generations of engineers. Britain's industrial might was built on structural and civil engineering, so Diggerland might prove in the long run to be a recruitment centre for tomorrow's construction industry. Of course, it will also inspire the eccentrics, and diggers have a pretty eccentric heritage. Joseph Cyril Bamford founded JCB in his garage with a £1 welding kit on the day his son was born in 1945. Some of the company's early models came with an in-cab kettle. Joe took great pride in presenting his customers personally with their JCB kettle. Another triumph for the great British brew-up.

Today, if you were of a mind, you could take up dumper racing, synchronised digger dancing or

Formula JCB. Yes, that's right – JCB makes a GT, a digger with a V8 Chevrolet engine, capable of doing 100mph. (*Britain's Wackiest Police Chases Vol 38* will doubtless be full of guttersnipes in stolen JCB GTs.) It seems that fans of diggers will do anything with their yellow friends. Diggerland may be just the beginning.

Orford Ness

The lonely places our technocrats choose for their
obscene experiments ... Again and again you'll find
these sick laboratories built on or beneath such
haunted sites.

David Rudkin, *Penda's Fen*

As you stand on the quay waiting to cross the River Ore to Orford Ness, you get the sense that you're not really meant to go there. It could be the cautionary crosswind that whips up from the coast in classic horror film fashion, or perhaps the ominous lack of a queue for the passenger ferry over the quiet stretch of water. Whatever the feeling is, it hasn't left by the time the ferry pilot abandons you on the island and starts his journey back. Your apprehension only deepens when a National Trust volunteer presents you with a small map and tells you – quoting the foreboding advice from who knows how many Hammer films – not to stray from the paths . . .

Like Kelvedon Hatch Nuclear Bunker (see page 34) Orford Ness is founded on fear. Throughout history, Suffolk's cliff-free beaches have been an open door for invaders. Countless Napoleonic-era Martello towers along the coastline and Orford's twelfth-century castle bear witness to the constant threat of attack from the sea. However, the best protection against invasion was formed 1,500 years ago by natural forces: Orford Ness itself.

The Ness is a National Trust-protected shingle spit, ten miles long and a mile wide. Its lanky, unkempt form provides a wild and picturesque barrier between the coast and the mainland. Formed by longshore drift, a process where the sea erodes rocks and carries shingle at an angle across the beach, its constantly shifting wetlands create the perfect habitat for many species of birds and wild flowers. However, the amorphousness of this landscape also provided the perfect soggy foundations for concealing one of Britain's best-kept military secrets. This was the place where Blighty road-tested bits of her atomic bomb.

Over the course of the twentieth century, from the moment the War Department withdrew the land from public access in 1913, through two World Wars and countless false alarms, Orford Ness grew countless new reinforced concrete features. Airfields, hangars, barracks and laboratories sprang up overnight as if planted by grey-fingered generals, small enough to go unnoticed from the mainland but large enough to house all manner of alarming machinery. Ironically most of the early construction was carried out by enemy POWs, erecting weapon- and aircraft-testing facilities that would hopefully give Britain the technological edge in future wars.

Although some non-destructive research was carried out on the Ness, such as Robert Watson Watt's early development of radar, it was mainly guns and explosions. The Lethality and Vulnerability trials of the 1940s and 1950s appeared to involve nothing more complicated than firing rounds of German ammunition at Allied aircraft in order to see what happened. Unfortunately, as weapons became more powerful, more complicated testing procedures were required, and greater became the need to conceal their existence from the public. We were never going to know what hit us.

Military secrecy, just as it did in the US in the 1950s, led to all sorts of outlandish rumours. Stories started to be told of UFOs and sinister experiments, none of which probably has any basis in fact. But retell a folk tale often enough, and it develops a subliminal power, so this haunting spit of land is the closest Britain gets to a Los Alamos, or an Area 51, all ghostly bad vibes and fantasies of Men From The Ministry shooing you away from something suspicious glowing under a tarpaulin.

Because Orford Ness sits on the very eastern edge of Britain, if the weather is anything other than blazing sunshine, it's worth making a few preparations before your visit. Don't forget to pack a Thermos of hot, strong tea, a pair of sensible walking shoes and an embarrassingly woolly hat. For two or three bracing hours it'll be just you with some hollow old buildings and the North Sea wind for company and it can get a little chilly. For the more adventurous, a pair of binoculars may be hung casually about the neck, but this should only be attempted after passing

Advanced Level Hiking and Twitching, and could be seen as a little over the top.

You'd also be advised to allow as much time for your trip as you can. Although the passenger ferry to Orford Ness leaves the mainland regularly between 10am and 2pm, the last boat back departs at 5pm. You wouldn't want to be caught there after sundown. It's scary enough in daylight.

There are three set paths around the Ness, whose accessibility depends on the time of year; the four-and-a-quarter mile Red Trail, the seven-mile Green Trail and the half mile Blue Trail. Three hours should be sufficient for the longest of the routes, but don't worry if you feel like you're rushing round and only glimpsing the surroundings. Only the fittest military historian-cum-conservationist will be able to absorb everything on offer and it's as much to do with what you feel as what you see.

On a quiet day the sense of isolation on the walk is incredible, only offset by the constant sensation of being observed. The police watchtower is now empty and most of the security fencing has been removed, but the spectre of military paranoia still enshrouds the beach. You suspect that you might be breaking the rules by simply being there. Besides, you're not going to want to stray from the visitor trails. The front of the guidebook highlights two important points: firstly, that the surrounding wildlife habitats are easily damaged and secondly that anyone straying from the paths is in danger from leftover bullets and bomb fragments. Now that's a proper warning. You wonder if they hand out the same guides to the avocets and seagulls before the nesting season.

Years of military history are being left to decay on the spit. Following the fading colour-coded walkways around the windswept, wildflower-covered pasture, you are surrounded by evidence of the constant battle between man and nature. Flowers force their way up between the paving slabs, refusing to lie dormant, stubbornly pushing through concrete. It is interesting to note that buildings designed forty years ago to contain a bomb blast should be so easily cracked open by the action of the wind and the sea. Walk towards the deserted barracks and a family of rabbits scatter. It's their home now. A part of one of the ugliest experiments in history may have occurred just round the corner, but it's Mother Nature who is having the final word – 'well, if you've *quite* finished playing with your bombs, I'll get on with some flowers, thanks'.

A picture-postcard red-and-white-striped light-house, designed to save life, nestles innocently on the horizon next to evidence of an aggressive past designed to destroy it – the sinister looking Labs 4 and 5, known to the locals as the 'Pagodas'. The silhouettes of these hat-shaped laboratories dip and loom just out of view on the horizon like two empty temples, dodging yet drawing the eye. Built in 1966 by the Atomic Weapons Research Establishment, there's much speculation about what munitions these build-ings would have tested, but we do know that their characteristic heavy sloping roofs (750 and 500 tons) were designed to collapse onto the building and contain any blast that may have occurred within. The pillars that still support the caps of the pagodas to this day suggest that, thankfully, this didn't happen.

Towards the far shoreline, the bomb ballistics observation building thrusts up out of the flatness like an Old Dark House. As you approach, you can hear the ghostly keening of a Bernard Hermann score, as if something horrible were about to happen. You stop to listen and realise that the tower is singing to you. The wind gusting over the Ness is playing the building like an Aeolian harp, producing a series of long, ever-changing chords from the metal framework of the stairs. It is at once beautiful and unnerving. It must have been the ideal place from which to view Blue Danube – the British atomic bomb which, with or without its nuclear core, was first tested on Orford Ness on Monday 6 August 1956 in Laboratory 1.

Lab 1 is just over half a mile from the ballistics building as the debris flies. The only one of the bomb test labs to remain open to the public (unfortunately this is where the path ends – you can't play on the Pagodas), it must win the prize for Bleakest Building on the Ness. A cavernous, decaying monument to Man's overwhelming need to blow things up, its hollow, roofless shell provides the perfect final mental image of the military's involvement on the spit. Shingle is piled high up its walls, designed to minimise any sideways movement during the bomb testing process. Its lightweight aluminium roof has long since gone.

Frozen in time exactly as it was after the tests, bar the scavenging of scrap dealers, without lighting or any attempt at restoration, it leaves the visitor in the dark as to what may have occurred within. We have to assume that the scientists wouldn't have been stupid enough to shake a live atomic bomb, but we do know that parts of the device, notably the detonator, would have been subjected to extreme forces within this building to ensure that they wouldn't go off accidentally in carriage. Nuclear or not, the charge would still have packed a devastating punch. Running a stress test on it must have been like deliberately shaking a hive full of highly explosive bees at arm's length.

A switch on the wall remains permanently rusted in the 'on' position. You can imagine the scientists arguing about who was going to go back in after the blast and switch the thing off.

As you return to the ferry, the military debris fades over the horizon and the marshland takes over. Turning your back on the grey architecture and heading back towards Orford, you rejoin civilisation. Paths you walked an hour ago take on a less sinister appearance through the haze of reeds. You can't help feeling a little sorry for the people of Suffolk. Just two years after the MoD left the Ness in 1985, and nuclear messing about appeared to have ceased in the region, construction began on Sizewell B power station a few miles down the coast. Maybe the seaside is so tempting because that way, if something does go wrong, you've only got neighbours on one side to complain about the noise. Whenever our need for power outstrips our understanding of how to control it, we'll build our testing facilities in these lonely places.

Exhibition Road

Wear your learning like a pocket watch and keep it hidden.

Lord Chesterfield, *Letters to his Son*

Unsung heroes can turn up in the unlikeliest places. For instance, two of London's least celebrated gems are hidden plumb in the middle of two of its busiest museums. Sometimes the best place to lose yourself is in a crowd.

The Wellcome Collection of medical history at the Science Museum is not to be confused with the expensive, flashy and modern Wellcome Wing in the same building, with its countless interactive buttons and virtual reality Ride-On Albert Einstein simulators (or whatever they'll have put in by the time this book is published). That's all well and good, but this emphasis on fun is hardly British. If you want an amusement arcade, go to the seaside. We want the history of science, and we want it done properly, with lots of darkened glass cabinets, slack-jawed skulls and bowls of leeches.

The Wellcome Collection is tucked away near the top of the building, the museum's mad relative in the attic. The best way to approach is up the back stairs to the fourth floor, past the aeronautical exhibits. Visiting during the school holidays, it's pleasant to slip round flight simulators and racks of historic sextants having touchscreens attached to them, and let the blaring hubbub of noisy, sugary fun fade away. The silence is quite eerie.

At the top of the stairs is a display cabinet that would be a surefire front runner in any list of Britain's great glass boxes. It's not even inside the main Wellcome collection, but it causes groups of children to scurry past it, sneaking a glance out of the corner of one eye and going 'euuurgh!' with exaggerated disgust.

There's everything you could wish for lurking inside. A dissected and dried human head? Check. A terrifying, snaggle toothed eighteenth-century merman made out of papier mâché and fish bones? Yes! Florence Nightingale's hair? Of course (though not all of it). With its mesmerising array of gnarled faces, empty eye sockets, wrinkled skin and jars of shadowy shapes, the cabinet acts as an enticing ballyhoo – 'roll up and witness the medical history freakshow'. All that's missing is a picture of a dog-faced boy and a scroll of elaborate painted lettering promising 'You Won't Believe Your Eyes'.

Although the gallery was only opened in its current form in 1981 (as a wonderful Binatone TV game typeface on the signage attests), its low lighting and occasionally grisly exhibits preserve all the *Elephant Man* atmosphere of a Victorian hospital storeroom. The label under a row of shrunken heads sums it up nicely: 'we've chosen some examples from our large collection of these heads'. It beats collecting stamps.

The oddness of medical equipment is a constant joy. A display of ancient Etruscan dental bridges sits near a beautifully preserved seventeenth-century brass nose, just round the corner from an arrangement of tonsil guillotines. Wax anatomical figures reflect the early nineteenth-century practice of studying the circulatory system by injecting wax into corpses' veins with specially designed syringes. Professor Gunther Von Hagens, who managed to shock everybody in 2002 with his queasy *Bodyworlds* exhibition, was clearly not doing anything new.

On one wall hangs a huge iron mortsafe – a protection against the bodysnatchers who supplied corpses for Von Hagens' nineteenth-century antecedents. The formidable cage would have been temporarily fitted round a newly buried coffin until the body had decomposed sufficiently to be of no resale value to the medical profession. It's a reminder that we only know how the human body works because centuries of naughty scientists have been cutting it up illegally against all the best advice.

Until the First World War, it soon becomes clear, the solution to all known ills was to saw the affected area off, drain it of blood, and see what happened. Exhibit after exhibit is dedicated to phlebotomy (medical bloodletting), from ornamental blood bowls to leech cages for bringing your worms home from the apothecary's shop. There's even a beautiful Iraqi bloodletting machine, spruced up with jaunty pointing puppets to indicate the number of armfuls drained.

The brutality of early medicine is numbing. A Georgian surgeon's kit is full of what look like lumberjack's saws and, as a sop to patient care, one of those round, semi-circular lumps of leather for the patient to bite. That's obviously the luxury model – down the scale a bit there are ugly boxes containing a single hammer. The progression through time of this equipment from the thuggish to the delicate is fascinating. By the late Victorian era you are marvelling at elegantly crafted boxes full of tiny spectacle screwdrivers and intricate pointy things, realising how far we've come. Yes, everyone wore pretty dresses in the olden days, but the most routine operation could end up like *The Texas Chainsaw Massacre*.

Medical history also appears to be full of people labouring for years to discover things you can't believe we haven't always known. It's worth reminding yourself that it isn't common sense that blood circulates round the body. William Harvey discovered that just 300 years ago. And it may seem obvious that flies and maggots just hang around near old meat because it looks so damn tasty, but for centuries it was assumed that the rotting meat actually created insects – bluebottles miraculously springing into existence within the mouldy bits of chops.

There's evidence of humankind's endless faith in new technology (descriptions of James Graham's eighteenth-century 'Celestial Bed' and its promise to cure impotence through electric shocks) and of the make-do attitude that needs to exist at the fringes of medical research (Joseph Lister carrying out sensitive bacteriological experiments in the sherry glasses from his sideboard because no specialised equipment was available). And if you're not strangely delighted by the Victorian admissions book for Bedlam Madhouse ('Reason for admission – Sudden Prosperity'), you need your head examined.

This is a serious, rigorous collection, but because it deals with something we all own – a human body – it's universally interesting. There's a certain sort of imaginative youngster who revels in blood, filth and mucus, and will walk over hot coals in search of smashed skulls and thirteenth-century leper skeletons. If you've got that sort of child, or just never grew out of that phase yourself, you'll have a ball.

*

Now cross the road to the Victoria and Albert Museum and pay a visit to their incredible Cast Courts. They may not sound particularly interesting on paper. They don't jump out of the museum guide at you like Tippoo's bizarre mechanical tiger organ, the Great Bed of Ware or Canova's *Three Graces*, all of which are fantastic and justify a visit to the V&A on their own, but let's face it – been that, bought there, done the t-shirt. No, the two Cast Courts are something a bit special and, once seen, you'll never look at sculpture in the same way again.

Unlike the Wellcome Collection's inconspicuous presence, hidden in the darkest corner of the continually modernised Science Museum, the Cast Courts aren't quite so neglected. They're as popular today as they were when they first opened in 1873, and because they take up two huge rooms and stretch the entire height of the building, they're pretty hard to miss. The reason for their inclusion in this book is that within a purportedly sensible museum, they're a precious oasis of Victorian lunacy.

Travel back, if you will, to the nineteenth century, when every self-respecting Englishman believed he had carte blanche to travel the globe and plunder whatever he fancied from the treasures of the ancient world. For a brief period it seemed as if the entire planet's artistic heritage was slowly making its way across the Channel by the boatload. This shameless cultural traffic was responsible for the current resting place of the Parthenon Marbles, the contents of countless Egyptian tombs and, more recently, Rolf Harris.

Like a pack of determined leaf cutter ants, hundreds of tiny top-hatted Britons scurried abroad, carved huge chunks out of historic sculptures, and brought them back home for display and artistic reference. In the days before package holidays, it was the most convenient way for the British populace to see the wonders of the world. And if the Greeks wanted to see the bits we'd torn off their beloved temple, well they could jolly well pay to see them in Elgin's shed like everyone else.

But there was an alternative to all this wanton pillage: taking a plaster cast of the desired object and bringing that back instead. It must have been a revelation in the early days of photography to be able to capture a three-dimensional likeness of your favourite sculpture, correct in every detail. Better still that your lightweight copy could then be broken into easily transported sections and carried home without upsetting the locals. Problem solved.

The Cast Courts contain the V&A's collection of these bizarre nineteenth-century replicas. Effectively European Civilisation's Greatest Hits, the two Courts are a glorious mess. Both rooms, although equal in proportion, show the imbalance of Victorians' artistic interest with one dedicated to Northern European and Spanish casts and the other solely to Italian replicas (the result of one too many Grand Tours, perhaps).

The main thing that hits you on entering the Courts is the sheer quantity of good-looking pieces of art crammed into the same room. An angel taken from the exterior of Westminster Abbey is dwarfed by a Czech statue of St George and the Dragon. Beautifully ornate casts of entire pulpits from European chapels, accustomed to being the centrepiece of a room, are rendered almost insignificant when surrounded by so much other splendour. The scale of the rooms and the overbearingly ornate decoration makes it feel like you're lost in Elton John's bathroom.

The mark of a great sculptor is the creation of something beautiful from unforgiving materials. It begins with the search for the perfect piece of marble, exactly the right size and quality, with no irregularities running through the grain. Then days are spent carefully lifting the precious stone from a quarry and manoeuvring it back to the workshop without damaging it. Then the virgin rock is worked, removing in order to create, chip by chip, knowing that one misguided blow could turn David into Davina. These plaster casts are to proper sculpture what paint-by-numbers is to painting. It's the ultimate Victorian hobby. Go abroad, see something you like, take a full-size plaster replica back home. You can imagine these casts being used like an early holiday slide show – 'We've found this magnificent little cathedral in Rouen. Had a spectacular forty-foot ornate arch over the main doors. Hang on a second, I'll just wheel it in.'

In fact, absurd as it may sound, the casts are very like holiday snaps. Anything that would fit in a camera's frame – tombs, celtic crosses or statues – is reproduced in its entirety. Anything bigger and the cast makers start to get bored halfway round, cropping the bits off at the side. Take the North Transept of Bordeaux Cathedral for example, reproduced in the North Europe court and ending abruptly halfway round the arch. Did the collector reach this point and then decide that maybe his 'entire cathedral' idea may have been a bit overambitious?

More impressive is the massive Pórtico de la Gloria reproduced wholesale from the cathedral of Santiago de Compostela. The plaster replication of the masonry is outstanding, its four arches spanning almost an entire wall. The casts of the cathedral doors under the arches, however, are from four completely different European churches, stuck in to fill the gap like some enormous Victorian Super Chapel. The Russian Doll effect of buildings within buildings within buildings is seizure inducing, but if you can manage it, do take a moment to admire the far right-hand door from the Augsburg cathedral in Germany, whose door knockers appear to be Statler and Waldorf from *The Muppet Show*.

A more familiar face and genitals can be seen in the Italian court. The towering twenty-foot-high copy of Michelangelo's *David* was originally a gift for Queen Victoria. The sovereign reacted as if she had been presented with a beautiful but unwieldy giant's shoe, and passed it on to the museum. To spare blushes during royal visits to the V&A, a plaster fig leaf was cast to hang over his crown jewels.

The centrepiece of the collection must, however, be the museum's cover version of Trajan's Column in Rome. Sawn in half so it can be fitted within the height of the building, it still towers twice to the ceiling. Any lessening of impact due to the halving of the monument is more than made up for by the excitement of getting to see the middle of the column in detail, something that would be impossible to do on the original unless you were touring the Eternal City on a pair of stilts. This is great for art students, but does raise questions about the nature of viewing a copy. Are you looking to see the details in the Victorian plaster casting (which must have been a job in itself) or do you look past that to admire the skill of the original craftsmen?

The huge cracks running up the side of Trajan's Column suggest that cutting the replica in half was a sensible idea, if only for safety's sake. The original column works because it's made of marble. In plaster, you're going to get a few problems. Bizarrely though, the replica is now showing fewer signs of wear than its Roman counterpart. Preserved in the V&A away from the elements and traffic pollution, details are visible on the fake which have long since faded on the original. Whether another cast will be taken from the cast to preserve what we have at the moment remains to be seen.

This is probably one of the major reasons to see the Cast Courts. As one of the few nineteenth-century collections of this type to have survived, it's not only a place where you can view a selection of some of Europe's finest works of architectural and sculptural excellence, but also a snapshot of artistic achievement, lasting long after the original may have decayed or been destroyed. The casts are only fragile plaster memories of how the pieces looked 150 years ago and, providing the mobile-phone-waving idiot who was wandering round slapping the pieces heartily during our visit didn't do any lasting damage, then they should be around for 150 years more.

Tebay Services

I think I could eat one of Bellamy's veal pies.
William Pitt The Younger, attributed last words

Once in a while, life is truly surprising. High in Cumbria, at the foot of the stunning Shap Fell, is a peaceful haven, full of good food and warm welcome. On a clear day, you can picnic amongst the ducks and cows. On a rainy day, you arrive through the mist, like King Arthur nearing Camelot. That such an oasis exists in one of Britain's most stupidly gorgeous corners isn't unexpected in the least. But this is a motorway service station. And that isn't just truly surprising, it's almost unbelievable.

When the M6 came thundering through John Dunning's farmland in 1972, he bid for the right to run a modest two-pump filling station and twenty-eight-seater café on the northbound carriageway and, just to prove that sometimes the best man wins, he got it. Today, Tebay is a thriving business across two impressive sites on either side of the motorway. Radio Four listeners (a singularly discerning bunch) voted it Britain's Best Local Food Retailer. If this sounds like some sort of wondrous dream, rest assured, it's all true. Tebay is what happens when you tear up the notion of the service station and start again from first principles.

Motorway services, as any fule kno, are among the vilest places on earth. They prey on the bored and the road-weary. Like airports, they are ugly traps laid for defenceless travellers where there's little else to do but unload rather too much of your money into the gaping tills of a parade of foul mockeries of shops and restaurants. If any of these godforsaken charnel houses had the good manners to hang warning signs over the entrances reading YOU ARE AN IDIOT you might forgive them for treating you that way. Since they don't, they deserve no mercy.

At the typical service station, the true horror of life slowly unravels before your red eyes. Picking your way through the McDetritus of the car park (where you are increasingly charged to park by the same mean sods who neglect it), you enter a nightmare world of fattening bleakness and costly misery. Like a condemned prisoner, you shuffle with your sticky tray past plastic-packed fruit, miniature drinks, arid pastries and myriad variations on prison slop growing thick skins under hot lamps. You have a below-average lunch with one drink and a pretend yoghurt for £13, without being able to summon the energy (before or after) to wonder how the entire contents of your plate could possibly be worth a penny more than £1.50. Annexes bleep, squeak and scream with slot machines. The last signature on the toilet cleaning rota is a fortnight old. The feeling of PMT (post motorway tristesse) is overwhelming. You have been cheated, sucked into a meretricious circus of sugar bombs, straggling Brownies and CDs of Ultimate Driving Ballads.

Tebay is about as many light years from this archetype as is possible. It is, in every respect, a complete pleasure. It is manned by humans with conversational skills, not an army of patronised part-timers pushing vending machine buttons on your behalf. The food is frequently organic, and either locally sourced or imported from specialists employing only a handful of workers. Even the ready meals meet these extraordinary criteria. The kitchen staff have been known to bring in their mums' recipes and make bestsellers of them.

The buildings are constructed from local stone, set in landscaped surroundings among some of the finest scenery in the country. The view from the restaurant tables isn't of cars and trucks, it's of hills and ducks. You're swaddled in the warm scent of fresh food, of baking and roasting, of wood and wicker. The farm shop bristles wall-to-wall with British cheeses, local lamb, wild boar, dressings, rare oils, herb jellies, rum butter, trucklements, fudge and biscuits. These are things you can buy, take away, and enjoy for months – something you'd be hard pushed to say about a scotch egg bar or a bottle of banana Frijj.

You won't come away from this maverick rest stop having stuffed the kids to the gunwales with tic-inducing additives, either. The last thing you need as you sit in a steaming tapeworm of traffic is your offspring bouncing off the headrests behind you.

Tebay flies in the face of the peculiar ethos of its market. It would seem obvious to suggest that, for a business to succeed, it needs at minimum to (a) satisfy a need, (b) offer a good product, (c) price it competitively and (d) serve it well. Most motorway services can avoid bothering with the last three because they don't rely on return custom, and are isolated from competition by miles of empty road. Only the lack of anything else makes you stop at most of these dumps, so it isn't surprising that they take the piss with such impunity.

In the early days of the service station, things were very different. Take Leicester Forest East, the midpoint of the M1, for example. Built in the mid-1960s to a radical design by the uncommonly British sounding Brian Leather, it followed the fashionable Italian model, bridging both carriageways of the new road. The ground floor transport caff, its air thick with cigarette smoke, was home to lorry drivers and young bikers tucking into egg, bacon and chips. Meanwhile – and fasten your seatbelts for this – the genteel folk of Blaby and Glen Parva would come specially for an evening out at The Captain's Table, the expensive restaurant (one of Terence Conran's first) on the bridge. They were greeted by the maître d'hôtel (an Italian dressed in a captain's uniform), shown to their table, and enjoyed silver service from waitresses dressed in navy blue and white. A cocktail pianist tinkled discreetly away in the corner. Glammed up diners studied the elaborate menu while enjoying a panoramic view of one of the country's greatest engineering triumphs, even if it was just six lanes of traffic.*

Tebay marks something of a return to Leicester's high ideals of fine food and civilised atmosphere, although thankfully without the stuffy formality or, for that matter, the cigarette smoke. Unlike so many hundreds of other pitstops, you would happily choose to return to Tebay, and plenty of people do. The restaurant's Cumberland sausage with stuffing and mash is the sort of sturdy, top-notch nosh that would make Rick Stein eulogise. Egon Ronay already

---

*The Captain's Table had a colourful history. A few weeks after opening, a gang of bikers escorting an empty lorry arrived, terrorised the staff, and stole all its furniture. The restaurant was later awarded five stars by the AA, and the accolade of being the most expensive motorway eaterie in Britain.

has. It is the sort of place you could go for a meal. It is the sort of place you could go for a hearty walk. The parent company, Westmorland, owns a caravan park and three-star hotel nearby, so it is the sort of place you could go for a whole fortnight of sausage, mash and hearty walks, should you fancy.

Just up the road is Westmorland's latest wheeze, Rheged, a remarkable underground visitor attraction centre that would need its own chapter to be properly described. At Rheged a cinema, a conference venue, art galleries, cafés, shops and the National Mountaineering Exhibition have all been built into an earth-sheltered space in a reclaimed quarry. It's hard to decide which is the more inspired bit of lateral thinking – putting a mountaineering centre underground or building a motorway service station that treats you like an adult.

Westmorland is an ambitious and original company which truly deserves its success. Next to any of its miserable rivals nationwide, Tebay is motorways ahead. It is vintage Stilton to their cheese spread triangles, Jamaican Blue Mountain to their freeze-dried instant coffee. It flatters the intelligence, the palate and the wallet. And it has its own telescope. (Beat that, Moto.) Unless Leigh Delamare Rest Stop turns into a butterfly this is the only motorway service station you can sincerely call a conversation starter. It is the exception to the rule, which is both a dreadful state of affairs and, to the frazzled driver on the M6, a gigantic relief.

Williamson Tunnels

Leave my wall alone. Last forever, that.
        Alan Bleasdale, *Boys From The Blackstuff*

For the connoisseur of unusual tourist attractions, Williamson's network of very big holes scores highly in three essential fields: being massive; being completely hidden from view; and being of no discernible use.

Joseph Williamson was born in 1769, one of the few facts we can definitely pin on the man. From humble beginnings, he worked diligently, married wisely, and rose to become the owner of the Tate

Tobacco and Snuff empire in Liverpool. Then, between 1805 and 1840 he dug a great maze of tunnels under the city for no good reason, and died, without leaving a single hint as to what on earth he was playing at.

Starting in his own street, Williamson and an army of local workers built an insane underground knot of passages. It's the sort of structure that would make Maurits Escher sit back and chew his pencil, before deciding to give up and find something easier to draw, like a nice vase of flowers or the central nervous system.

Under Liverpool's Edge Hill district, where the council offices and University accommodation now stand, are tunnels upon tunnels, vaults within vaults, casements and staircases, tangled like Christmas fairy lights in a bag in a loft. Archways sit at ninety degrees to one another, and passages plunge deep into the ground at colossal scale then scurry off sideways as tiny drainpipes. Williamson entertained people with full dinners down here and, after the death of his wife, reputedly became a virtual underground recluse, and nobody really knows why.

From the tiny scraps of information we have, Williamson comes across as a private and eccentric man. He wore a 'shocking bad' hat and tatty clothes, but scrupulously clean underwear. And, in common with fellow Merseyside construction visionary William Hesketh Lever, who chose to sleep outdoors (see the chapter on Port Sunlight) he shunned the humdrum bedchamber, spending his nights in a room described as more of a 'den for a wild beast than the dwelling of a human being'.

But he was clearly sane enough to become a pillar of society. Although he was at pains to stress that the tunnels were not a 'showroom' nor he a 'showman', he didn't let slip exactly what they were supposed to be. If the project were nothing more than a high-spirited joke or the work of a lunatic, it would perhaps be easier to dismiss. Yet the tunnels are there – scrupulously constructed, mad, useless and simply enormous.

The full extent of the tunnelling still remains to be discovered. Despite maps, geophysical surveys, historical accounts and good old-fashioned hacking into the ground with spades, the modern curators of this attraction are only beginning to scratch the surface. Though Williamson's folly was never forgotten as such, it is only since the mid-1990s that any sustained attempt has been made to reclaim it from dirt, collapse, and most importantly, the contents of hundreds of years of Scouse dustbins.

The residents of Edge Hill started shovelling their refuse into Williamson's chambers almost as soon as he had stopped building them. The practice was so widespread that in 1867, the excellently titled news-paper *The Porcupine* claimed the tunnels were 'an evil . . . and a gigantic nuisance' – probably on account of the fifteen feet of sewage lying in the cavities under Mason Street. By the 1930s even the massive Banquet-ing Hall chamber beneath Williamson's house was classified as unsuitable for use as an air raid shelter because it was so full of shit.

Luckily times change. Plenty of clearing has taken place in preparation for the opening of the tunnels to the public, and the modern visitor is not required to stroll through rubble and dung at any point. But as you enter, the raked entrance tunnel does drop away towards an excavation pit, revealing that the passage is twice as deep as it first appeared. What you thought was a stone floor is in fact just compacted Victorian rubbish.

The first impression is that the mind behind this project was very easily distracted. There is no sense of order. Stepped brick courses run halfway up crazily angled arches then just stop. Keystones are slammed in upside down and wedged with bits of brick. Symmetry and perspective take the day off. Even the huge arch that provides the front view of the attraction has another arch stuffed inside it for good measure. It is simultaneously a haphazard mess and an industrial marvel. Imagine a cross between an action painting and an aqueduct.

According to contemporary accounts, Williamson was not the sort of man who really understood what shape things ought to be. Even the houses he built above ground appeared 'as if built by chance . . . as if a blind man has felt his way . . . large rooms and small rooms and queer passages oddly running out'. He equipped his houses with windowless and floorless rooms of wildly inappropriate sizes. If this was what Williamson chose to show the world, imagine what the stuff he hid underground is like. His tunnels are naughty architecture, an absent-minded doodle come to life.

The gleeful confusion Williamson left behind is reflected in the dumbfounded awe with which the tunnel guides describe their workplace. The attraction is staffed by enthusiasts, many of whom, when they're not shining torches for tourists, are crouching elsewhere in the site reclaiming long-lost chambers with a spade. There is a sense of continuity in the way that the people of Liverpool are now redis-covering the unusual marvels which their ancestors may have built.

The tunnels were opened to the public less than a decade ago. Local fascination as to what lay under their doorsteps was such that 3,000 visitors turned up on the launch day to see just ten yards of tunnel, and the organisers had to turn people away. This inquisitiveness may stem from a fascination that we can have so little knowledge of something this huge, which was built so comparatively recently.

We genuinely know almost nothing about the tun-nels. Williamson had no blueprints and was notori-ously secretive about what he was doing at the time. The oldest surviving accounts of the works date from years after his death. They describe a visit by local historian James Stonehouse, who, reeling and bam-boozled, described man-made caverns and whole underground houses we have yet to discover. Even in 1845, barely five years after building work had ceased, the place was already a real headscratcher. Stonehouse marvelled that the site appeared to be 'utterly useless ... We have stupendous works without perceptible motive, without plan, meaning, reason or form'. So what on earth was going on?

Several explanations have been put forward, all of which are feasible given the lack of evidence. Perhaps the rich but socially aware Williamson was just giving work to people who needed it. Liverpool in the early 1800s was bursting at the seams with recently demobbed soldiers from the Napoleonic Wars. Building lots of pointless tunnels would have been good regular work for anyone willing to swap his rifle for a pickaxe. According to legend, when the supply of willing workers outstripped the work that needed doing, Williamson would tell labourers to dig a hole at one end of the works, then swap them the next day with another team at the other end of the site who would fill it in again. The man himself denied any philanthropy on his part, but he may just have been sustaining the façade of the pragmatic businessman.

Certainly the training he gave was useful, and many of his tunnel builders went on to work on the great railway projects of the North West. They also scared the living daylights out of Robert Stevenson's navvies, who broke through into Williamson's works by accident while constructing the Lime Street rail tunnel, causing many of Stevenson's workers to flee, convinced they'd tunnelled down into 'the devil's kingdom'. Seeing the berserk constructions for yourself, you may sympathise with their assumption.

Another suggestion is that Williamson and his wife may have been members of one of the apocalyptic religious sects then flourishing in the city. Certainly, some of the tunnels have church-like features and gothic-arched casements that might be suitable for a religious retreat. Perhaps Williamson was planning an underground hideaway where he and a short list of his chosen people could sneak off while the battle of Armageddon raged overhead, only to emerge later and build a new Merseyside Jerusalem, presumably with lots of arches at odd angles and upside-down staircases.

Some local historians are now speculating that Williamson was not building tunnels at all, but rather shoring up the miles of holes left behind from the ancient sandstone quarries of Edge Hill. With his seemingly slapdash arrangements of arches and vaults, he may just have been trying to reinforce the ground so he could build more houses on top. This idea that he wasn't a tunneller as much as an arch builder at least partly explains the anything-goes architecture of the site, but the whole enterprise remains a higgledy-piggledy monument to what happens when you try and build an underground city of vaults without any blueprints.

The mystery only makes a visit to the tunnels more exciting. This is a unique and fascinating attraction for the same reason ancient stone circles are. Someone put a lot of effort into building this, and we have no idea why. When people start telling us aliens built the Pyramids or Stonehenge, just because we can't find a clear account of why or how it was done, it's worth reminding yourself we haven't got a clue what the Williamson tunnels are for and they're not much older than *Pride and Prejudice*.

We like to think we're pretty smart, with our twenty-first-century hair and our trainers with lights on, but most of the stuff we know is just stuff someone else found out and told us. We only 'know' history because somebody wrote it down and someone else passed the information on to us. Faced with a monumental structure with no accompanying written records, historians and archaeologists have to shrug their shoulders and keep digging, and we, as laypeople, just have to look at the thing open-mouthed and open-minded. The Williamson tunnels are a good example of how fragile our knowledge of the past is, of how easily stuff can be forgotten – how mysterious the world of only a few generations back can be if we lose the receipts.

Barometer World

Ten minutes of this rain will do more good in half an hour than a fortnight of ordinary rain would do in a month.

Jack Rosenthal, *Wide-Eyed And Legless*

If there's one conversation we British love having about the weather, it's the conversation about how often we have conversations about the weather. Barometer World, therefore, ought to qualify for a Britishness award, for its services to social intercourse. Ambrose Bierce's *The Devil's Dictionary* defines a barometer as 'an ingenious device for telling us what kind of weather we are having.' But, as Philip Collins, the big cheese of Barometer World (and probably the world of barometers) will tell you, he was wrong. Barometers, unlike us, aren't interested in the weather. They measure atmospheric pressure.

Don't be too deflated by this. You'll still be hard pushed to pass a barometer without your eyes alighting on the word RAIN. Even if a barometer doesn't care how cold or windy it is, it still flirts with the idea of being a wall-mounted Michael Fish. Without its contribution to our understanding of 'the wonderful ocean of air in which we live', weather forecasts would be the stuff of a sci-fi writer's fevered fantasies.

Of course, the thing about barometers is that they require human input. They're useless unless you know the previous reading. In that respect, you may as well look out of the window. But, like the Mini, the red telephone kiosk and the London Underground map,* they're one of those happy meetings of science

*Respectively designed by Sir Alec Issigonis, Sir Giles Gilbert Scott and Harry Beck, in whose debt we languish. This annotation is the publisher's entry for next year's Great British Footnote awards.

and art, of function and ornament, of engineering and craftsmanship.

Barometer World is unusual in so many respects. At first it appears an unremarkable place, but as you near the entrance, you suddenly find yourself standing next to what looks like an enormous upturned eggcup with windows. Collins, it turns out, is learning to blow glass, so he's built himself a wood-fired seventeenth-century glassmaker's kiln, one that reaches temperatures of 1,200° Celsius and takes two days to cool down. You don't mess with someone who owns a six-foot furnace.

This, says its proprietor, is not a museum: it's an exhibition. He's being modest. It's three things: a shop, a workshop and a display space for the Banfield collection – 349 barometers on permanent loan from the family of the same name. You can admire these but you'll have to memorise your favourites. Though photography is allowed in the shop and workshop, snaps of the Banfield collection are prohibited because it's categorised by insurance types as 'price-less'. There's really nothing to compare with it. There was a barometer museum in Holland, but it's gone now, so Barometer World stands well and truly on its Tod.

Something else that's gone now is Finisterre, one of the hypnotic stars of the shipping forecast. In 2002, the Met Office renamed Finisterre in honour of its own founder, Admiral Fitzroy, former MP, second Governor of New Zealand, captain of HMS *Beagle*, and therefore the man who took Charles Darwin round the world so he could think about where we came from. Fitzroy (the man to whom the atmosphere was a wonderful ocean of air) established the Met Office in 1854 for the benefit of his fellow sailors, thus institutionalising Britain's favourite national conversation. The reason we mention the redoubtable Admiral is that he has the unique distinction of lending his name to not only a sea area but also a type of barometer.* Here at Quicksilver Barn, there are dozens of Fitzroy barometers in walnut, rosewood, mahogany and oak hanging on the walls. No MDF model yet, but it can only be a matter of time.

There's something very quiet and clinical about

---

*He also gave his name to a mountain, a river and a South American conifer. A deeply religious man, Fitzroy was tormented with guilt over the part he had played in the development of Darwin's anti-creationist ideas, and eventually took his own life in 1865.

the exhibition, which feels almost uncomfortably reverent. There used to be information boards scattered about, but Collins removed them because nobody read them, which is a shame, because it's a pretty baffling collection to the atmospheric novice.

Happily, it's also just the slightest bit bonkers. In the middle of the collection is a glass cylindrical chamber containing a lot of carefully wrought brass and a dozen leeches. This is a magnificent £20,000 re-creation of Dr George Merryweather's Tempest Prognosticator, Or Atmospheric Electromagnetic Telegraph Conducted By Animal Instinct, shown at the Great Exhibition in 1851. A 'jury' of twelve leeches is provoked by changes in atmospheric pressure to slither towards the top of the bottle where they cause traps to activate hammers that strike bells, warning you of bad weather. Sounds complicated. Is.

The Leech Barometer raises a lot of smiles, alongside the occasional squeamish snarl, and is rightly the star of the show. It's an insane piece of work, but as his giant glassblowing furnace proves, the curator is an unstoppable whirlwind of similarly ambitious schemes. If it involves glass or air pressure, he wants to give it a go. In 2000, Collins reconstructed the famous Magdeburg experiment (the seventeenth-century one where horses try to pull apart a pair of vacuum-sealed copper hemispheres), and that's without even mentioning the replica Victorian vacuum train he built that went so fast that it crashed.

Collins, you won't be surprised to learn, is no stranger to television (except in the sense that he doesn't own one himself).* He impressed Adam Hart-Davis on one of those BBC technical history jamborees, and he even made it on to *The Big Breakfast,* where Johnny Vaughan admitted privately that he owned a barometer, but wouldn't confess to it on air. Chicken.

Why anyone might feel the need to hide their barometer under a bushel is baffling. Until fairly recently, barometers were an essential feature of any respectable hallway. They would often form part of a wall set, along with a clock, a thermometer, a cameo picture of the cliffs at Dover, a brush set, or, very often, a mirror, so you could adjust your hair and make-up after being blown about by a storm you'd been warned was coming but had still gone out in anyway. Because

---

* Sad, really, since the cathode ray doodah at the heart of every television is a sealed glass vacuum tube, which you reckon would be right up his street.

their mechanism is so simple it barely warrants the term, barometers tend to last an awfully long time, dangling steadfastly near the coat rack from decade to decade, as reliable and unchanging as glowering grey clouds in a Bank Holiday sky. That's not to say all barometers are happy with a safe, indoor life. Ever wondered how tough explorer types measure the height of the mountain they've just climbed? Why with a tough explorer's barometer, of course.

So perhaps it's time you had a barometer. There are plenty in the shop, from the familiar wooden dial design to some stunning but unfathomable glass sculptures that look like they were designed by Björk. Even if your relationship with atmospheric pressure is limited to a cursory 'nice day!' with the woman from next-door-but-one twice a year, you might be surprisingly tempted to become a fully paid up member of the barometer-owning community. After all, Johnny Vaughan* is.

*On our way to visit the Shah Jahan Mosque (see p 106), we were kept waiting behind the taxi from which Johnny Vaughan was alighting outside his home. It was sunny at the time, with patchy cloud and highs of about 13° Celsius, as Johnny would have found out when he walked into his hallway and consulted his barometer.

Portmeirion

Before you let the sun in, mind it wipes its shoes.
Dylan Thomas, *Under Milk Wood*

Almost uniquely amongst the attractions in this book, Portmeirion is very famous. It's even famous in the modern sense of the word, in that it has been on the telly. But, like a venerable Shakespearean actor who only gets pestered for autographs because he once played a scenery-chewing baddie in a Hollywood blockbuster, it's worth looking beyond Portmeirion's screen role to get the best out of it.

Naturally, you wouldn't expect to get more than

two paragraphs into a piece on Portmeirion without mention of *The Prisoner,* Patrick McGoohan's 1960s exercise in audience head-messing. Portmeirion was pressed into service, almost untouched by set-dressers, as The Village – the sinister, ice-cream-coloured community where men in Aarnio chairs took turns trying to annoy McGoohan's shouty spy so much he'd go mad. The stylish look of the programme, which owes a fair amount to Portmeirion, makes it one of the few cult fantasy shows that you can admit to liking in polite company without being required to spend the rest of the evening in the shed. It's a good programme. If you like it, you should go to Portmeirion. It'll blow the top of your head off.

But if you don't like *The Prisoner,* or haven't seen it, or don't have a television, or are allergic to Patrick McGoohan, you should still go to Portmeirion, because if we let the cult TV enthusiasts have this place to themselves, they'll pop a little flag with a penny farthing on it in the top of the bell tower and declare it property of the fan club. And that would be a pity, because Portmeirion would still be worth a visit if it had never been on telly at all.

Portmeirion is an idealised Italian village, blended into a chunk of the Welsh coast so seamlessly that for a moment you are persuaded that this is exactly where Italian villages ought to be. The man behind what must qualify as Britain's most impressive folly was Sir Clough Williams-Ellis. Born in 1883, Williams-Ellis was a pioneering environmental campaigner, self-taught architect and spirited idealist who wanted to prove that sticking a man-made structure somewhere beautiful needn't necessarily mean ruining the place.

Like anyone thinking of building a Big Train Set, Williams-Ellis originally wanted an island to play with, looking as far afield as New Zealand. He eventually found the perfect site less than five miles from his family home, when, for £5,000, his uncle sold him the Aber Iâ peninsula in Snowdonia. Williams-Ellis renamed his new acquisition Portmeirion ('-meirion' from the county of Meirioneth). The name is a deliberate echo of Portofino in Italy, whose combination of a beautiful setting ornamented by appropriate architecture Williams-Ellis considered a model for what he called an 'experiment in sympathetic development'.

In 1926, Williams-Ellis opened the peninsula as a holiday resort, making a hotel out of the one suitable building that stood there. The food was, by his own admission, diabolical, but the pretty coastline and the balmy Gulf Stream climate had the fashionable set pouring in, and soon he had enough money to start doing something delightfully silly with buildings.

From the outset, tourism was a necessary part of the fantasy town's economy. The architect considered this suitable vengeance for a slight delivered to his ancestor Gruffydd ap Cynan, the twelfth-century King of Wales. Gruffydd's castle on the peninsula had been knocked down by Sir William Fothergill Cook (inventor of the electric telegraph) for fear that it 'might attract visitors to the place.' One can only hope that Cook is turning and beeping in his grave.

The first stroke of the pencil was the Bell Tower, sketching in the main feature of the town in preparation for the frenzied scribbling to come. This was a bold statement of intent, showing that something unusual was planned – after all, not many Welsh villages are structured round a campanile. Williams-Ellis later explained that 'it was imperative that I should open my performance with a dramatic gesture of some sort.' Portmeirion, from the very beginning, was architecture as theatre.

Portmeirion is a stage set, which is probably why it looks so good on screen. *Trompe l'oeil* features are painted on every wall. Even the public toilets are slathered with flat urns and crevices-that-aren't. Two- and three-dimensional sculptures sit side by side. Nothing is as big as it looks, with an arsenal of tricks deployed to fool you. Walls tilt inward using forced perspective. The windows on the first floor are a fraction of the size of the ones below. Even the paint fades in tone as it gets higher up the walls to boggle your depth perception. It's only when you stand close up that you realise a house that seems to be vanishing into the clouds is actually no higher than a bus. Anyone seen comfortably exiting a Portmeirion house through an archway was probably in the cast of *Time Bandits*.

The playfulness of the architecture is a world away from the austere nasty-medicine attitude of many modern architects, who often seem convinced they're doing the public good by not explaining themselves properly. Williams-Ellis wanted to popularise his craft. He described his style as 'light opera', and there is something decidedly Gilbert and Sullivan about the town planning. It wouldn't surprise you if pirates and admirals started trilling from the balconies as you passed. Portmeirion is frothy and fun, which makes it approachable; the often arcane science of architecture (which after all is something we all have to live with every day) is rendered accessible for the layperson.

Williams-Ellis understood the general public's relationship to buildings – he himself had only a few months in the ivory tower of formal training before he swanned off the London campus at the age of 22 and opened his own architectural practice. So it's no surprise that his attitude to building owed little to the cold world of the planning office. Almost nothing here has sprung from a 'proper' architect's drawing. Williams-Ellis sketched roughly what he wanted – the silhouette of a dome, the shape of a gatehouse – and left it to his trusted craftsmen to get the details right. (The Bell Tower is one of the few structures to have been made from thorough half-inch plans, which is a relief as otherwise it would probably have fallen on someone's head by now.)

Not to denigrate Williams-Ellis' enormous skill and craft, but imagine a whole village built by the sort of dad who spends Sunday afternoon in his garden shed turning some broken bits of armchair into a magazine rack. Portmeirion is the work of a benign Frankenstein, cannibalising leftovers from other buildings to make new ones. Its architect referred to the village as a 'home for fallen buildings.' The impressive colonnade in the main square was transported stone-by-stone from its original home in Bristol, the Bell Tower clock was salvaged from a London brewery, the porch of the Pantheon is an old Norman Shaw fireplace, and the iron grille stuck to the front of the Town Hall was once part of the Bank of England.

The distinctive panels of mermaids that appear all over the village were rescued in 1954 from the old seamen's home in Liverpool before the bulldozers moved in. These were particular favourites of Williams-Ellis and turn up everywhere – one even ended up as far afield as Knightsbridge in London, attached to what was once the Portmeirion antique shop in Pont Street. This scavenging of random architectural heritage keeps the site from becoming a slavish pastiche of Italian design. Instead the village is a celebration of all sorts of building styles, from the gothic to the Georgian, pressed together in surprising harmony with each other and the Welsh cliffside.

During the near fifty year period of construction at Portmeirion (between 1926 and 1972, with an interval from 1939 to 1954 when fighting and austerity stopped play) Williams-Ellis would buy bits and pieces of old buildings, then find uses for them, sometimes decades later. The fantastic Gloriette in the village centre is made of broken bits of Hooton Hall in Cheshire which, by the time Williams-Ellis remembered he had them lying about somewhere, needed to be dug up from a garden which had been laid over the top.

The process of turning an ordinary building into a Portmeirion one was referred to by the architect and staff as 'Cloughing up.' All around you is evidence that the village was built with one man's love, reflecting one man's obsession. At the age of 80, Clough Williams-Ellis could be seen shinning up a ladder to gild the dome of his Parthenon. By the time of his death at the age of 93, he seems to have been content that his village was fairly complete (barring a planned Lion Tower which he never got to put up, meaning there's probably a pile of unused lions somewhere).

The estate is in good hands; the list of trustees is a family tree heavy with Ellis progeny. He passed on hoping his descendants would continue to give his village 'little presents', and they have – adding such features as 1983's gazebo erected to mark the centenary of the architect's birth, employing another handful of those mermaid panels.

Although the Italian influence is obvious, there is an unconquerable whimsical Britishness about this place that goes deeper than the incongruous Welsh signage screwed to the Mediterranean pastel-wash walls. Perhaps the unique charm of the project is best summed up by William Brodie's imposing statue of Hercules which Williams-Ellis bought and erected between the main plaza and the Town Hall.

The Victorian sculpture looked as if it needed something to commemorate, so a plaque was put up recording that Hercules was erected in honour of 'the glorious summer of 1959.' A matching plaque from 1973 records the architect's disgust at that year's poor summer. Summers were important to Clough Williams-Ellis – so much that he even erected an astrolabe in the village in honour of William Willett, the man behind British Summer Time. What could be more British than building a Utopia where statues don't commemorate wars, battles and other noisy dramas, but the small triumphs and disappointments of the weather?

By the way, if you are travelling to Portmeirion as

a fan of its televised incarnation, please be warned that the one house you really want to see – Patrick McGoohan's billet as Number Six – no longer looks quite like it did in the series. It has been filled with calendars, had its frontage jazzed up and been turned into a *Prisoner* gift shop to cater to demand from fans. So you've only yourself to blame. Don't worry. Swallow your disappointment and go and celebrate Clough Williams-Ellis instead. He really did refuse to be pushed, filed, stamped, indexed, briefed, debriefed or numbered. He was a free man.

Edinburgh Camera Obscura

Any sufficiently advanced technology is indistinguishable from magic.

Arthur C. Clarke, *Profiles of the Future*

In our world of plasma televisions and camera-phones, the visual novelties which boggled the eyes of our parents and grandparents can seem a bit simplistic. We no longer make pinhole cameras out of old biscuit tins – possibly because biscuits now come unhelpfully packaged in floppy wrappers – nor do we run screaming from the Odeon multiplex, convinced that a black-and-white cattle stampede is about to trample all over us to the accompaniment of jaunty ragtime piano.

Back in 1982, the front cover of the *TV Times* tried to rekindle our awe. We were about to welcome in a new age of three-dimensional telly courtesy of *The Real World*, ITV's not-at-all-like-*Tomorrow's-World* science show. The coming revolution momentarily caught the public imagination, with thousands rushing to buy a special issue of the magazine with free cover-mounted 3-D glasses. As families (who had only bought one copy each, naturally) jostled for possession of a manky bit of white cardboard with a couple of coloured celluloid squares stuck to it, the promised leap into a stereoscopic future turned out to be a lot of items falling straight towards the camera in an oscillating blur that suggested someone really ought to nip out on the roof and have a fiddle with the aerial.

But for one brief moment, we were prepared to overlook the fact that this was the same technology that had last been rolled out to make monsters lurch at 1950s teenagers. And even now, in a century that we were told would have us all commuting to the planet Mongo in atomic wheelships, the average *TV Times* reader still feels no nearer the era of three-dimensional weathermen, no matter how wide their screen. Museums full of Victorian stereograms will attest to the fact that 3-D photography is practically as old as photography itself, and we're still not very good at it.

But as that experiment proved, it's never too late to dust off an old trick for a new audience. Handled well, old technology can still feel like the future. Take the *camera obscura*. Edinburgh has got a lovely one, and it has persistently wowed paying audiences for more than 150 years.

A basic *camera obscura* was designed by Arabic scholars in the tenth century (as a means of viewing eclipses), making this a millennium-old entertainment. Portable models are thought to have been used by artists such as Vermeer and Canaletto (making every primary school teacher who traces a picture onto the whiteboard from an overhead projector heir to a grand tradition of artistic cheating). Predictably, Renaissance cleverclogs Leonardo da Vinci had time to sketch one himself when he wasn't too busy designing helicopters.

In the nineteenth century there was a vogue for sophisticated, public versions that attracted paying customers. While only a mere handful of functioning examples remain in the UK, this was the cinema of the Dickensian era. They were typically erected overlooking the country's more pleasing areas; there's one near the Clifton Suspension Bridge just outside Bristol. Another was built on the Welsh coast by Sir Clough Williams-Ellis, and a further example in Sussex by 'Mad Jack' Fuller within his eccentric observatory (see the entries on Portmeirion and the Sugar Loaf, where neither has been mentioned).

To make a *camera obscura,* you need a darkened chamber – the literal translation of its Latin name – topped with a tower fitted with a mirror and a few lenses.* The device enables a paying punter within the sealed chamber to watch the world going about its business, projected, seemingly by magic, onto a white viewing table. Commanding the outside world to appear as miniature moving images on a flat horizontal surface must have left spectators then, as now, with a feeling of Olympian omniscience.

The illusion is as beguiling as it ever was, needing no hi-tech makeovers to drag it into the modern age. The conspiratorial atmosphere of a bunch of

*We didn't pay attention in physics lessons and we're not about to start getting interested in meniscus lenses now.

strangers gathering in a darkened room to spy on an unwitting Edinburgh is almost cabalistic. This is the closest thing to a session of crystal ball gazing that you'll find, especially if it's not a clear day when you make your visit. A couple of simple tricks, probably as old as the Camera, are performed by the guide with a piece of white card: hoisting pedestrians aloft like a bored god is particularly impressive.

The whole experience lasts around fifteen minutes. It's incredibly simple, highly memorable and a little bizarre. You've just been entertained by a hollow pole with a couple of twisty bits – science that hasn't been new or cutting edge for several centuries, yet still leaves you with a caveman-trying-to-understand-broadband expression on your face. You've gazed at reality reproduced on a white table with far more awe than you have ever gazed at actual reality. Downstairs, it's just cars and people and shops and buildings. From up here, using your magic seeing-table, it's the unwitting world of tiny mortals, and it's yours to spy upon. Ha ha ha! Thankfully you'll walk away without the sense that someone has charged you a fiver to stare at their bicycle through a periscope; although the science involved is about as basic.

As you step blinking back into daylight, take a stroll round the exterior balcony and let your eyes adjust to looking at the city below without the aid of jiggery-pokery. Gameboys are abandoned as kids beg their mums and dads for 20p, wanting to have a go on the coin-operated telescopes. The wonders of the *camera obscura* have distracted them from all that electronic guff. Anything with lenses is suddenly a must. Take advantage of it; you know it won't last.

On your way downstairs, check out the rest of the tower, which is filled with optical illusions. Most date back a generation or two, but exhibit the same reluctance to surrender their modernity as the *camera obscura*. For instance, although the things were invented in 1949, and there's one on your bank card, one of life's purest pleasures is standing in front of a hologram, rocking your head back and forth and trying to see round the back. Like photocopiers, most of us still don't have a clue how they work, so you're allowed to be impressed.

Everywhere you look, there are trick pictures, 3-D images and complicated arrangements of oddly shaped mirrors. Soon you're dizzy from an overload of stereograms and kaleidoscopes. Your mind hurts and in a minute you just know you're going to be looking down the holographic eyepiece of a hologram of a microscope to see a hologram of a microchip. And don't turn round – there's a laser-rendered Boy George behind you. The relief of finding something as reassuring as a simple Mona Lisa in a frame is brief. Just as you get your bearings from a familiar face, you register that her head is made out of rabbits. You want to tell her to calm down, that she's just showing off.

The last thing you need to come across on the stairs (so you inevitably do) is a carefully placed print of Escher's inescapable staircase. Suddenly you're trapped in the kind of mind game usually only tackled by Diana Rigg in a leather catsuit. It's all part of the fun though. Surviving this experience with your sanity intact is as satisfying as winning a game of Scrabble using the Z, the Q and both Fs on a triple word score.

Despite its shiny new appearance this is a grand collection of Victorian fairground ephemera, New Age folderol and 1960s hippie nonsense. Imagine the walls of a maths student's college room, newly decorated with posters bought during Freshers' Week – fractals, optical illusions, 'magic eye' images, anything with intellectual rather than aesthetic appeal; they're supposed to be cheering the place up but all they manage to do is make you fall over.

Though it uses every trick mankind has ever learned about eyes, this is one of the simplest forms of entertainment. Like sniffing paraquat or eating mature cheddar, however, it's probably best not to engage in this sort of activity just before bed. The brain won't stop fizzing for hours after a rare work-out like this. Although almost everything here is done using technology that is decades if not centuries old, it continues to draw appreciative, smiling, excited crowds. We still want to be fooled and entertained by all the old tricks. Perhaps we don't need 3-D television after all.

Crystal Palace Dinosaurs

A grin was on the face of the monster.

Mary Shelley, *Frankenstein*

Originally built 150 years ago, but reopened in its current form in 2004, the Dinosaur Tidal Lake at Crystal Palace cleverly earns itself a place as both one of the oldest and newest attractions in this book. Over its lifetime, these prehistoric monster statues have seen fashions come and go, but right now, thanks to a decade or so of computer generated films and television, dinosaurs are as hot a property as they were when the place was built, when the only way to see iguanodons was to come to Penge.

It is a truth universally acknowledged that dinosaurs are brilliant. Strictly speaking, of the sculptures built for this display, only a handful are technically dinosaurs, the rest being Ichthyosaurs (the fishy ones), pterosaurs (the flying ones) or prehistoric mammals (the furry ones). On the other hand, your inner child only wants to know about dinosaurs, so for the purposes of this chapter – yes, there are loads of dinosaurs.

The sculptures were commissioned when Crystal Palace Park was laid out as a permanent home for the leftovers from the Great Exhibition of 1851. Fossil mania had been raging for decades, and it was decided that Penge Hill would see its ancient landscape re-created in stone. The work was commissioned by park mastermind Joseph Paxton, and carried out by Benjamin Waterhouse Hawkins under the direction of Richard Owen, the renowned anatomist and leading British dinosaur expert of the time. Although he was a staunch anti-evolutionist (insisting that every animal, live or extinct, was handcrafted by God) history has ensured that Owen's surviving monuments, including the Natural History Museum in London and these imposing statues, are many people's first face-to-face encounter with the concept of evolution. He must be furious.

Although Crystal Palace is one of the world's greatest dinosaur parks, don't go expecting tacky Hollywood spectacle, animatronic velociraptors and laser-lit dinoramas. Any updating of the site has been done in the spirit of sturdy Victorian values.

The internet has several ratty missives posted on it from disappointed Americans who have crossed the Atlantic expecting some sort of Dinosaur Disneyland. Tough. This is British, and it's made using big, stone statues, a few clumps of trees and your suspension of disbelief.

Excitingly, the new landscaping has created space for many statues formerly relegated to the park storerooms. Visitors now travel backwards in time past family groups of extinct mammals – massive sloths and extinct camel-things scurrying amongst the half light of the trees – before getting to the sexy reptiles. The budget also stretched to adding some models intended for the original exhibit but never completed, all freshly crafted from Hawkins' blueprints. For the first time, a gang of pterosaurs can be spotted curling their leathery wings from a rocky outcrop above the lake.

The statues may be frozen stock still, but visit at sunset and the play of shadows brings everything to life. The mosasaur peeps its head from the watery depths, showing off the contours of a skull the Victorians had only just dug up, while cleverly refusing to reveal a body about which they didn't have a clue. The iguanodon clambers up a tree stump, its mighty forelegs cocked like a circus elephant. The stone wizardry tickles the imagination, a real temptation for parents to whisper to their kids, 'that one just winked at you'.

The new look, with its low wooden fencing, jungle bridges and woodchip paths is a witty way to make the place feel like a modern wildlife park ('Can we go to the dinosaur zoo, mum?') but the Victorian flavour remains. Monsters have even been placed back on examples of the geological rocks from which their bones were hacked by nineteenth-century fossil hunters, just as the original designers intended.

The statues' colours have also been restored to Hawkins' muted palette of olives, greys and browns. For many years the park was cared for by a warden who painted the monsters in *Yellow Submarine* hues, all mauve legs and white toenails. It may just have been his attempt to make them stand out amongst the tangle of trees from which they used to cower. Now, thank goodness, for the first time in decades the models are all visible, facing outwards towards clear walkways (with the exception of the hylaeosaur, who is currently pointing his buttocks at everybody for some reason). Anyone who visited before 2004 and wondered what all the fuss was about ought to go and have a look at what's been done with this place.

The development reignites the excitement that must have been felt when the dinosaurs were first displayed – an occasion that so thrilled Britain's scientific glitterati that they celebrated by having a publicity-friendly eight-course dinner in the belly of the iguanodon (or more accurately its casting mould). *Punch* magazine, which had sarcastically christened the park's glasshouse centrepiece 'The Crystal Palace' in the first place, wryly noted that 'had it been an earlier geological period (the guests) might have occupied the Iguanodon's inside without having any dinner there.'

Of course, any schoolchild dinofan could tell you that iguanodons eat plants, not scientists. But it wasn't just comic magazines who were making elementary dinosaur howlers at the time. The supposed experts weren't much better. The whole exhibit is not so much a commemoration of cutting-edge science, as a reminder of soon-to-be-abandoned ignorance. The beasts are enormous and beautifully made, but they're almost all wrong.

Iguanodons weren't lumbering, rhinocerine tanks. They stood upright and browsed like giraffes. The spike that the palæontologists proudly stuck onto the statue's nose was actually the animal's horny defensive thumb. Labyrinthodons don't really look much like frogs. Just about every prehistoric beast that had ever been discovered by the 1850s gets a model here, but palæontology was in its infancy at the time, and it shows. As far as accurate re-creations of dinosaurs go, most of these statues might as well be of that irritating purple character who teaches children the alphabet.

The park is a relic, an example of science trapped in amber. Because the monsters are classified as Grade I listed buildings, they cannot be altered, only restored. So we have a stone snapshot of the state of knowledge in 1854. It's worth cherishing. The preservation and display of scientific ignorance doesn't happen very often. You might see the odd map in a museum that still tries to persuade you that the stars revolve round the earth on a crystal sphere propelled by giant mice or something, but this is in a whole different league.

The people responsible for *Walking With Dinosaurs* should be forced to spend a day at Crystal Palace. Presenting current scientific ideas using state-of-the-art reconstruction turns vague theories into solid-looking reality, bypassing any awkward questions from the viewer – 'It's real! Look! We've built one!' – but it's a trick, and it's nothing new. It's what the sculptors at Crystal Palace did more than a hundred and fifty years ago only with cement rather than computers. And doesn't that confidence look silly now?

Science is at its best when it's up for debate. Teach children that we didn't always know something and they begin to think they might have a chance at working stuff out themselves, that there may be a point studying the subject. All science starts as supposition. That's an empowering thought.

This beautiful park's finest function is as a reminder that knowledge, like animals, evolves, that one year's absolute truth is the next year's laughable nonsense. Only forty years after the park had opened, celebrated American palæontologists Edward Cope and Othniel Marsh visited the Crystal Palace dinosaurs and, barely disguising their giggles, declared that, 'There is nothing like unto them in the heavens or on the earth,' which is late Victorian for 'Your dinosaurs are rubbish. You're making it up.'

So it's a little disappointing that this unique aspect of the park is not explained properly at the moment. There are no plaques or display boards telling visitors about the fascinating context of these wrong monsters. If you want to teach your children about the folly of scientific confidence, you'll have to do it yourself. Bromley Council, who were responsible for the recent restoration, are keen to put more educational material into the park but claim that they have simply run out of money – and energy – to put the project through.

It's surprising to discover that, if you phone the restoration team and try and compliment them on the work, it takes a fair while to persuade them you're not playing an elaborate trick. Apparently nobody calls them to be nice. The first unveiling of the sculptures in the 1850s predated the publication of Darwin's *Origin of Species* by almost six years, and caused outrage. It seems that the restoration of them has had the same effect.

The dinosaurs are unfortunately part of an ongoing row with the local residents over the redevelopment of the entire park. The initial proposal was to raise private investment by giving planning permission for a grotesque-sounding multiplex cinema and bowling alley on the site of the old Crystal Palace itself. When local opposition rightly stalled the plans, the dinosaurs found themselves the last part of the redevelopment project still proceeding, and funds soon ran dry.

Unfortunately, the bad taste of the original (and obviously horrible) proposals remains in many local mouths, meaning that the marvellous job done in the dinosaur corner has been tainted by association. It probably didn't help that the landscaping was masterminded by Kathryn Gustafson, architect of middle England's slippery *bête noire*, the Princess Diana memorial fountain. This has led to resistance to any further work on the monsters, with many locals deriding the whole restoration project as inappropriate for the environment.

Though it's understandable that residents are protective of their beautiful monsters, it's hard for an outsider to see the statues' careful repair and reinstatement as anything but a magnificent improvement.* As recently as 2000, scientific historian Deborah Cadbury was mourning these 'once proud trophies of a newly discovered science, chipped and broken, their paint long since faded, monstrous gargoyles, peeping out at the twenty-first century from rampant undergrowth, a bizarre reminder of forgotten hopes.' Now the choking foliage is gone the new presentation is awe-inspiring. A beautiful and well-intentioned project, it would be great to see it completed properly as a monument to scientific history.

Maybe it's our typical national distrust of the showy that has convinced some of the naysayers that the new dinosaur display is inappropriate, too slick and brassy, but that's a terrible overreaction to a great restoration job. It would be a tragedy if the residual ill will towards the original redevelopment plan should sully the potential for this bit of the park. If public support and finance could be found to

---

*Compare the botched job they've made of building a faux-Crystal Palace canopy on the Crystal Palace railway station. It looks nothing like a Victorian glasshouse. It turns the beautiful ironwork into the roof of a 1980s shopping precinct. That's how bad heritage restoration can be.

complete the job with full educational facilities, it would create a real reason for people to visit Crystal Palace. And with a few more of those nobody would have to suggest building a multiplex or a bowling alley in the middle of it ever again.

House of Marbles

Get thee glass eyes.

William Shakespeare, *King Lear*

Riding high in the list of Things Most Uncomfortable To Kneel Upon, alongside Lego bricks and upturned drawing pins is the humble glass marble. There's no contest. A plastic brick has only twelve edges to dig into your knee, a drawing pin a single point. A marble, being spherical, has an infinite number of unyielding surfaces. Every time a new generation of children discover marbles, a new generation of parents wonder how these colourful objects can be so easily overlooked when scrambling on all fours for the remote control.

Slap in the middle of a craft park – the exciting new name for an industrial estate that doesn't contain van hire or car tyre specialists – and housed in the beautiful 200-year-old buildings which were once home to the Bovey pottery, House of Marbles is a fantastic example of how a traditional industry can be presented to the public. Don't be misled by the frankly upsetting *trompe l'oeil* mural on the building's outer wall depicting jolly skeletons and a headachy recursive image of a woman painting a painting. It's not a very accurate guide to what's inside.

Founded in 1990, the House of Marbles is a perfect microcosm of the manufacturing, retail and leisure industries. The place creates, sells, amuses, educates and feeds in equal, effortless measures. There is a glassblowers' workspace, gift shop, massive marble run, museum and restaurant to visit, not to mention the glass-finishing areas and landscaped gardens (under construction at the time of writing) as well as the pottery buildings and kilns themselves. You can't say that you don't get value for money. Particularly since it's free.

The shop is so full of marbles, toys, games and

delicate glass objects within easy reach of excited childish hands that even the most optimistic parent will start reaching for the cheque book in fevered anticipation of breakages. If you've ever wondered what would happen if a bustling toy store like Hamley's introduced a glassware department, this is it. It says much about the organisation of this place that the owners only record two customer breakages a year. It's all extremely hands-on for somewhere that probably shouldn't be. The shop assistants must have nerves of steel and balls of glass.

Although the mixture of toys and cut crystal is initially bewildering, the blend works. There can't be many places where, under one roof, dad can pick up a traditional backgammon set, mum can get that Farting Cowboys board game she's always wanted ('Pull my finger, Sheriff!') and gran can attempt to complete her seemingly never-ending collection of tumbling glass clowns.

And then there are the marbles. Thousands of sparkling, multicoloured pieces of glass form a wonderful, 1950s Ladybird book illustration of a display, that is justifiably the centrepiece of the downstairs toyshop. The marbles, sold by size rather than weight, are not in fact made on site, but rather imported from China, Mexico and India – the daddies of modern marble production. Do supervise small children around the display, however, because even though signs are placed around the shop with the warning 'Caution: these are glass nuggets, not sweets,' the overflowing shelves do rather resemble a lethal pick 'n' mix counter.

Even though the marbles themselves might not be home produced, a large proportion of the other stock is manufactured on-site or locally. Many of Bovey's older residents will be ex-employees of the pottery and so there is a palpable sense of local interest and pride in the enterprise. It is encouraging to see a recently built themed-attraction producing a sense of pride in local craftsmanship rather than just loads of noise and litter.

The upper level of the shop is dominated by a gargantuan Rowland Emett esque metal sculpture bolted to the wall. This is Snooki, the brainchild of eccentric Swiss schoolteacher and mad sculptor Alex Schmid, and is probably the world's largest marble run. Built over a period of three months, during which time Schmid worked in a tent on-site and slept in a local B&B, the contraption looks like a perverted extension of the building's pipework. When switched on, which you can do by pressing a spherical button fixed to the balcony, it comes alive in a quite staggering fashion.

Instead of using glass marbles, which Schmid realised would break on a run of this scale, Snooki uses pool balls, about thirty of them in total, all sprung into clunking circulation round its intricate skeleton when a punter kicks the thing into action. The balls are carried on runs, slopes and loops; thrown against pool ball Newton's Cradles and traps; dropped into counterweighted baskets, cages, drain-pipes and eventually a large copper funnel at the bottom where they spin slowly down, only to be returned to the top by lift. Start it up and it sounds like a beach full of clockwork orangutans attempting to erect iron deckchairs. Apparently the staff notice the silences between each run more than the run itself.

The only thing oblivious to the noise appears to be Snoring Bear. Reclining on the upstairs counter he's nothing more complicated than a large teddy bear with a mechanical gadget inside that makes his chest rise and fall, accompanied by a tape of snoring. Although simple, the illusion proves utterly convincing for the under twelves; House of Marbles' website has a page dedicated to the slumbering bear where children can send in pictures that they've drawn for him, and he can sleep at them.

While children aren't being captivated by this ursine layabout, they can entertain themselves by not sitting on the two huge marbly marbles in the downstairs exhibition. Initially created by House of Marbles as a fun and ergonomic seating area for small children while they watched the three Alex Schmid mini marble runs on display, Boring Health and Tedious Safety officials have since decided that the two fantastic-looking seats should be accompanied by a cold 'Please do not sit on the marbles' sign. Hopefully there is a circle of hell reserved for people like this where they are forced to run with scissors on a loose carpet for all eternity.

The House of Marbles' small museum is currently looking after one of the biggest marble-making machines (and easily the most well-travelled) in the world. Weighing in at sixteen tons, it was custom made in America and once produced the world's largest machine-made marbles (about 1.4 inches in diameter). During its working life it churned out fifteen million marbles and travelled 10,000 miles, moving from West Virginia to Washington State, back to West Virginia and then finally to Britain, despite being so large that a wall had to be removed from the potteries to get the thing into the building.

If you visit during the week (or some Sundays) you can watch the Teign Valley glassblowers making glass things. Glassblowing is a deft and delicate skill. Grabbing purcellas, pontil irons and gobshears, the blowers form impossibly complicated new forms from sticky-looking balls of molten glass. Walking round a raised walkway safely away from the furnaces, you'll see glass bubbles blown and fantastic shapes appear from the molten sand. It's like an extreme sports balloon animal routine.

This is why House of Marbles really succeeds. Almost everything here is open to the general public and shown in its full glory. From the beautifully judged lighting throughout the building (essential for somewhere full to the gills with glass) to the open workshop floor, there's no attempt to hide the bits that make it all work. With glassblowing, like many traditional industries, the manufacturing process is every bit as fascinating as the final product itself.

Dennis Severs' House

The 'sampler' that the eldest daughter did at school will be spoken of as 'tapestry of the Victorian era,' and be almost priceless. The blue-and-white mugs of the present-day roadside inn will be hunted up, all cracked and chipped, and sold for their weight in gold, and rich people will use them for claret cups; and travellers from Japan will buy up all the 'Presents from Ramsgate,' and 'Souvenirs of Margate,' that may have escaped destruction, and take them back to Jedo as ancient English curios.

Jerome K. Jerome, *Three Men in a Boat*

In a bustling corner of London, a minute's walk from Liverpool Street station, is a street that, even if you know the area well, you've probably never stumbled upon. Sandwiched between Commercial Street and Bishopsgate, two areas full of skyscraping, glass-fronted redevelopment and people who eat money sandwiches for lunch, Folgate Street remains refreshingly overlooked. It's appropriate then that this road should hold one of London's greatest hidden treasures.

From the outside, 18 Folgate Street looks like an unremarkable four-storey Georgian town house. To the right of the ivy-framed front door sit two black sash windows, their red painted shutters hanging welcomingly open. Push your nose to the glass, and you'll be able to make out the front room, gloriously dressed in late Victorian splendour with its two caged canaries cast into silhouette by candle and firelight. It's an unusual scene for the early twenty-first century, particularly since no-one lives here any more.

Look closely and you'll find other clues that this is no ordinary residential address. There's a lit candle in the outside lamp and a list of opening hours subtly pinned to the front door, but chances are if you hadn't been warned there was something unusual about the place, you'd walk straight past. That's the thing about Dennis Severs' house. As the house motto puts it, 'you either see it or you don't.'

In order to understand the property, it's important to realise that the house isn't particularly significant historically. And even though it's decorated in a mixture of Georgian and Victorian styles, Mr Severs was born in 1948. And was from California.

Severs was an artist, and moved to London when he was nineteen. He was also an Anglophile, whose fascination with the traditional British way of life had led him to carve out a living during the 1970s running horse-drawn carriage tours round the West End of London. When his stables were demolished to make way for a new building development, he was forced to lay down his reins and move on.

In the late 1970s, looking for both a new project and somewhere to live, Severs headed to East London and bought the house in Folgate Street, Spitalfields. At that time it was not a desirable location, and properties there did not command the seven-figure price tags that they do nowadays. For Severs, the house wasn't an investment as much as a blank canvas. It was also in the arty East End, a stone's throw from the treasure trove of antique rubbish that is Brick Lane market – perfect for satisfying his love of period bric-a-brac.

Unlike most of the capital's period home buyers, Severs' vision wasn't one of re-plastered magnolia painted walls, William Morris scatter cushions and wet rooms (although there was a serious damp problem on the third floor). Instead, he was going to celebrate the property's lack of modernisation and embrace a more traditional way of life. Not in a carting-his-own-produce-to-the-local-market-in-his-Land-Rover-Discovery type of way. He was going to go the whole hog – with no electricity, no heating and, most terrifying of all, no lavatory.

Rather than limit himself to one period style, he decided that every room would reveal a further chapter in the property's history. It's a bizarre but effective conceit. As you explore the building from the early Georgian cellar and kitchen to the late Victorian attic, time seems to accelerate. It's the bricks-and-mortar equivalent of that cinematic device where a calendar spins into view and has its pages torn off.

Dressing each room with appropriate fixtures and fittings from his vast collection of antiques, Severs' house began to take shape. Some items that he felt were necessary for the feel of a room were prohibitively expensive so, in true DIY fashion, he built them himself from affordable scraps and cheap offcuts. Walking round you'll find that in places the decoration is less Georgian, more Bobby Georgian.

This isn't to say that the final effect is in any way tatty. In fact, the knick-knack cluttered rooms and the blend of mahogany and MDF continually remind you that this isn't a museum but a loving facsimile of how the house may have appeared a couple of hundred years ago. Legions of elegantly refitted stately homes have taught us to expect that every mantelpiece ornament be priceless and all paintings be by old masters. Severs' house forces us to relearn how to react to such objects.

The real Georgian inhabitants of 18 Folgate Street wouldn't necessarily have decorated their entire house with up-to-date Hepplewhite or Chippendale. A few fashionable centrepieces may well have set them back a bob or two, but a lot of the furniture would have probably been older, spruced up with oriental wooden trim to mirror the fashion of the time. The modern equivalent is dad sawing the lion's feet off gran's wardrobe to get it into the bedroom.

Dressed from floor to ceiling in fake history, the house also has fake inhabitants. Severs created the

Jervis family, fictional silk merchants who might have lived in such a property at the time. The Jervises were an essential part of the story he wove as he showed visitors round his home, and they continue to bring his house to life as you walk round today.

Thankfully, Severs spared us the embarrassment of stage school hopefuls in dented top hats following you round spouting pantomime pearls of Cockney wisdom. That you never actually encounter the Jervises makes the experience far more effective. But the evidence of their occupation of 18 Folgate Street surrounds you. Coffee sits, freshly brewed, in a pot on the stove. The fragrance of recently baked cakes fills the kitchen. The sheets on the four-poster bed in the master bedroom are left unmade. Clues about the family are there in sight, smell and sound, but you have to utilise all your senses to unravel the story.

For example, on arrival you are told, very politely, to keep quiet. Walk round the house in silence, as Severs intended, and you'll realise why. Hidden motion detectors trigger taped sound effects wherever you walk. Leave a room and you'll overhear people talking just out of sight, children laughing and distant church bells ringing. Make any sort of noise and you'll ruin the atmosphere. There is the unnerving impression that you've constantly just missed the inhabitants.

There are numerous light-hearted notes left around the house. Some remind you not to pick up or examine anything, some give pointers towards things to look out for, some give wry observations on the nature of what visiting 'heritage' houses is normally like. These take the place of Severs' original personal tour and indicate the spirit in which you're encouraged to enjoy the surroundings.

Tiny in-jokes reveal more of Severs' intended tone. Rotting bales of silk stand upon the top floor landing with delivery notes addressed to 'Masters Gilbert and George' and 'Mr (Dan) Cruikshank' (art luminaries and local friends of Dennis) while the cartoon Victoriana of the 'Sssh!' sign by the entrance to the withdrawing room blows away any suspicion of a stuffy atmosphere.

Art installation rather than heritage attraction, the house charts the fortunes of the family through five generations. The candle- and fire-lit interior which appears so cosy and opulent on the lower floors, gives way to piles of rubbish and dusty fireplaces as you climb higher through time and the family's fortune collapses. You really feel for the fake Victorian family renting the top rooms amongst all the genuine damp and decay of the building, left as it was when Severs bought it.

These last two rooms show the true Dickensian London, miles away from cartwheeling milkmaids and cheeky barrowboys, where taxes were paid but you got precious few public services in return. A filthy blanket sits under a table. It's not the dog's bed, but that of a crippled child. In the days when cholera and typhoid were believed to spread through the air, Londoners simply closed their windows tight and stayed in drinking infected water. Severs' warts-and-all approach confuses visitors expecting to see a chocolate box version of British history and rewards those with an open mind (and a shut mouth).

This is an anti-attraction, one which gets better the emptier it is of visitors, and the proprietors realise this. You won't find brown-and-white road signs directing you from the M25. There's no street sign advertising its presence. All you get is the sheet of printed A4 on the front door to explain that you're at the right place.

Nor are the opening hours designed to make things any easier. The house is open only six days a month for a few hours at a time. Although this means that you'll probably have to plan the day around your visit, the benefit is that everything is freshly prepared on your arrival. The food, smells and set dressing differ each time and are laid on as if you are a treasured guest, just as if Dennis himself was showing you round.

Severs died in 1999 leaving his house to The Spital-fields Trust who now maintain it beautifully. It's ironic, but testament to Severs' ingenuity and eye for detail that the fictional history of a make-believe silk merchant's family feels more believable than the genuine history of real families exhibited in stately homes throughout Britain. And thanks to the notes he left round the building, it feels as if Severs, like the Jervis family he created, has been absorbed into the fabric of the property. He remains in the home he built like a friendly ghost haunting his favourite spot. You'll turn a corner and feel you've just missed him, too.

Not everyone would have been able to live in the way that Dennis Severs did at 18 Folgate Street. Anyone accustomed to twentieth-century luxuries would have found the lack of sanitation and basic luxuries a shock to the system. However, the viewpoint it gave him into how his property would have functioned is integral to his vision and lends the fictional history and genealogy a definite air of authenticity. Just make sure you take advantage of the toilet in the pub opposite before you arrive.

Bletchley Park

Time is a changeable ally.

Winston Churchill, radio broadcast, 1940

Bletchley Park is rapidly approaching national treasure status. Its vital codebreaking role in World War II, for so long shrouded in obsessive secrecy, only became public in 1974, but is now common knowledge. Scores of column inches, books, television documentaries, plays and even a feature film have told the tale of the battle against the dreaded Enigma machine, the sinister-looking hybrid of typewriter, telephone exchange and gearbox used by the Germans to scramble their wartime communications. A regular stream of visitors come to learn more about this excellently curated site, surely the only part of Milton Keynes to warrant the adjective 'interesting'.

And it's a story worth celebrating. The Enigma was a fiendish device – you'd have more chance of winning the national lottery jackpot 11,000,000,000,000 times* than cracking its code once. It was a terrifying monster to overcome, but the frighteningly clever people at Bletchley Park did it. As a result, they shortened the war by two years, and our debt to them is immeasurable.

But this isn't the whole story. What's often overlooked is that to beat these stupidly difficult odds, to do the stacks of donkeywork and the unbelievably hard mathematics, these eccentric and brilliant mathematicians and engineers had to invent something we now take for granted – the computer.

Many people are credited with siring the computer. Victorian visionary Charles Babbage is probably the earliest genuine claimant, but in terms of

---

*That is, eleven great big British billions or 11,000 silly little American billions.

what we now understand as a computer's function – running programs, carrying out tasks for us, being plugged in, crashing, that sort of thing – this is where it all started.

Alan Turing, a brilliant young Cambridge mathematician, had come up with the idea as an intellectual tool in the 1930s. He proposed that a 'Universal Turing Machine' (the name didn't catch on, sadly) could receive a menu of mathematical operations, carry them out, store the information step by step, and cough up a result. His proposal would have sounded like conceptual piffle to many of his contemporaries, but he was right, and this description of the computer is still accurate today.

The word 'computer' comes from the word 'computor,' meaning 'one who adds up.' All any computer does is a lot of very fast sums. Whether you're deleting invitations to enlarge your debts and consolidate your penis, or bidding for a Kenny Everett action figure on eBay, Alan Turing made all this possible. Even so, we should be grateful to him.

Along with other first-class minds like codebreaker laureate Dillwyn Knox, Turing ended up as part of the Government Code and Cypher School, the forerunner of GCHQ, based at Bletchley Park –

codename Station X. The handsome estate eventually housed 10,000 employees, working in the glum-looking huts and blocks you can still see today. A few of these are currently home to some appropriately sympathetic small businesses whose windows you can peer through while visiting the site, including a PR company and, delightfully, a lab full of people messing with microwaves.

There were two significant computers developed at Bletchley. The first, a machine devised by Turing, was called the Bombe. This was a leviathan the size of two double wardrobes, one side covered in noisily spinning alphabetical wheels, the other side a dizzying mass of blood-red spaghetti – hundreds of small things wired to hundreds of other small things which helped crack the Enigma codes.

The other Bletchley computer, Colossus, was an even bigger beast, the size of a room and dedicated to defeating Lorenz, the Germans' giant new Enigma variation with four times as many fiendish alphabet-scrambling rotors. An evolution of the Bombe and incorporating ideas from the Universal Turing Machine, but with the speed-enhancing addition of 1,500 valves, Colossus was built by Post Office engineer Tommy Flowers, Bletchley's other great hero.

What Colossus gave the world was programming – in the words of Turing's biographer Andrew Hodges, 'the ability to mechanise the word IF.' Unlike machines that can only do one task (such as adding machines or peppermills), the two-and-a-half ton Colossus could make decisions based on rules, enabling it to do almost anything the Bletchley crew might ask of it.

Colossus, thanks to a characteristic British faith in innovation, nearly didn't get made at all. Valves were costly and regarded as unreliable by top brass, who were worried that they'd be spending 'a fortune on a giant electrical Christmas tree.' So Tommy Flowers raided his piggy bank and put a then-whopping £1,000 of his own money towards the project. How he explained this to his wife (who wasn't allowed to know what he was up to) is anyone's guess. To cut Bletchley's long story short (and you probably know the ending anyway) Britain invented the computer and we won the Second World War here.

One of Bletchley Park's great triumphs as an attraction is that many of the wartime staff have come back to lend a hand showing people round. If you're lucky you might hear first-hand accounts of Colossus's paper tape whizzing past at 60 mph – faster than most cars of the day – and the almighty mess it made when it snapped. Or the first ever programmable computer's popularity with the winter night shift, because the valves got so lovely and hot. You might hear about the Wrens drying their laundry on it.

This is, surely, British spirit at its finest. Here is the single most significant invention of the twentieth century, something which now has its footprint on practically everything we do, having socks hung from it. My, how little our attitude to the computer has changed. And my, how we dropped the ball.

It won't surprise you to learn that the book in your hands, like most things these days, was put together with help from American computers running American software. But, had a generation of British engineers not been sidelined by a lack of vision and a stack of bureaucracy, the computer on your desk or in your lap might have been made by English Electric, British Tabulating Machines or GEC. The Brits, it turns out, were at least two years ahead of the USA by the late 1940s – a huge head start – and this was largely thanks to Bletchley.

A world run by British computers – ah, the thought. We'd be running programmes, not programs. We wouldn't have to quit or exit, we'd TTFN. Teen spods of the 1980s would have been taking their first steps in Queen's BASIC:

```
10 PRINT "MARTIN IS ACE" PLEASE
20 GOTO 10 PLEASE
30 THANK YOU
```

But the Americans picked up the ball we dropped, squashed it into an American football shape, ran off with it to strike a home down (or whatever it is they do), and became computer champions of the world. But ever was it thus. Babbage, a man about as ahead of his time as it is possible to be without growing jet engines on one's elbows, wrote in 1852 that any brilliant new idea put to an Englishman will prompt him to 'find a difficulty, defect or an impossibility' where an American will 'find some new application of the principle, some new use for the instrument.' And to think no-one turned up to the man's funeral. Perhaps there weren't many Americans in town that week.

After years quietly marketing itself as the home of codebreaking, Bletchley Park has now embraced its part in the history of the computer with energetic élan. Not only can you see rebuilds of the mighty Bombe and the mind-blowing Colossus, but there's an entire room of ageing – sometimes vintage – computing technology. There are some truly bizarre machines amongst the collection: the New Brain, the Sportel (for that important part of office life, playing squash) and the Friden 123, a calculator that looks like the dashboard of a Citroën concept car. There are gigantic hard drives the size of Mini engines shelved above piles of phone books illustrating how much data they could hold (sometimes not much more than there is between these brackets).

This collection, along with memorabilia, assortimentia and some boggling information placards ('the possible Steckers such as R<->S1 can be exploited by the diagonal board') is housed in Block B. The Bletchley Park Trust is steadily and deliciously renovating the place at the moment, and there's more and more to see with each visit. Hut 8, Turing's home at Station X, is next in line for the decorators.

Of course, you can buy an Enigma keyring and a

cipher handkerchief here, but it's the extraordinary, eccentric history that makes Bletchley such a damned good egg. The codebreakers who worked there were a motley crew of academics, mathematicians, chess champions, crossword enthusiasts, Egyptologists, anthropologists, palæontologists and lawyers. There was also a marine biologist, given the job by mistake because he was an expert on cryptogams, which are nothing to do with code at all, but something to do with algae.

Many of the codebreakers were recruited through the inevitable old boy network – appropriately, since Bletchley Park sits halfway between Oxford and Cambridge. Great minds tend towards unconventional lifestyles, so don't be unduly alarmed by the stories of the man who threw his coffee cup into the lake rather than wash it up, or the man who wore a blue pixie hood on his ginger beard during winter.

Turing himself had a tea mug – a scarce commodity in wartime – which he guarded by chaining it to a radiator with a combination lock. Perhaps this was deliberately naive on his part, but when you're working amongst people cracking codes with odds of 159,000,000,000,000,000,000,000 to one, a three- or four-figure combination isn't going to take them very long, and Turing's precious mug was often nicked by his tittering colleagues.

All this eccentricity may have been a human response to the terrible pressure and relentless secrecy. One couple who met and fell in love at Bletchley admitted that, even after sixty years of marriage, neither of them knew what the other had been doing there. Thankfully for us, the geese that laid the golden eggs for Churchill have for some time been free to cackle all they like. Tommy Flowers helped the Trust reconstruct Colossus in the 1990s (from memory, as he'd destroyed all his plans after the war, as requested) and started to accrue his due recognition before his death in 1998. Not such a happy ending befell Alan Turing who, convicted of the crime of homosexuality in 1952, was sentenced to undergo psychiatric treatment and 'organo-therapy' – i.e. female hormone implants, which made him obese and rendered him impotent. He committed suicide two years later, at the age of 42, by taking two bites from an apple he'd dipped in cyanide.

The particular manner of Turing's farewell was inspired by a scene in Disney's *Snow White And The Seven Dwarfs*, coincidentally, another technical innovation of the time. In turn, his final act is said to have been the inspiration behind Apple Computer's corporate logo, although this story is mired in myth. Romantically, it would be a fitting homage if true – which means it almost certainly isn't. But his and Station X's legacy is without comparison: together they saved the lives of thousands of servicemen and secured the future of the country while quietly inventing the most significant machine ever known. Not a bad result, that. As the Trust's patron The Duke of Kent puts it, Bletchley is 'the place where the modern world began.' We should shout it from the rooftops. Or maybe e-mail it as a PowerPoint presentation.

Ripon Tramp Museum

There was nobody inside but a miserable shoeless criminal, who had been taken up for playing the flute, and who, the offence against society having been clearly proved, had been very properly committed by Mr Fang to the House of Correction for one month; with the appropriate and amusing remark that since he had so much breath to spare, it would be more wholesomely expended on the treadmill than in a musical instrument.

Charles Dickens, *Oliver Twist*

When it came to picking places to visit for this book, several criteria needed to be satisfied. Was the place unusual? Did it deserve greater publicity? And, as a bonus, did the name make us laugh? When one enthusiastic source suggested that Ripon was home to a Tramp Museum, we set off straight away, giddy with thoughts of dioramas full of bag-shoed Chaplinesque mannequins clutching sun-faded cans of Tennents Super. It was with some disappointment that we discovered that our source was misled. Ripon does not, after all, have a Tramp Museum. But it does have a Workhouse Museum, which has tramps in it. Well, *had* tramps in it. Even better, it also has a Prison and Police Museum, and a Courthouse Museum – and all three are within 500 yards of each other.

Given that Ripon's actual City Museum closed in 1956, it's miraculous that there are any museums here at all, let alone three, all on similar subjects and all shoulder to shoulder. The Ripon Museum Trust was set up in 1983 to preserve the city's history and, within a year, the previously empty police station had reopened as the Prison and Police Museum. Ten years later, the trust managed to acquire the old Ripon Union Workhouse and had soon converted it into what we are stubbornly going to continue calling the Tramp Museum. The final piece in the jigsaw was the Court Museum, opened in the old courthouse in 2000. Ripon museums were suddenly springing up from nowhere like Starbucks franchises.

The much-anticipated Workhouse (or Tramp) Museum is the best place to start. Local architects William Perkin* and Elisha Backhouse's grand Dutch-style Union Workhouse is a million miles away from the expected soot-caked Dickensian hellhole. The elegant main building, originally a shelter for the elderly, the infirm and the insane was briefly used as an old people's home in the 1950s and fittingly is now the headquarters of Ripon's Social Services. The museum itself is inside the single storey building opposite, the old 'casual wards'.

The workhouse would have provided shelter for two main types of inhabitant; 'casuals' (proper outdoors tramps seeking food and shelter for the night) and 'residents' (non-proper tramps with permanent accommodation). Up to twenty tramps would gather daily in a cottage (now flats) opposite the gates and

*Not the same William Perkin who accidentally invented mauve in 1856.

share a pot of very weak tea whilst they waited for the workhouse to open. At four o'clock they would form a queue, before being taken into the wards, checked for alcohol, stripped and cleaned with carbolic soap. The museum uses the same reception area as the original wards, and if that's the sort of thing that floats your boat, you could always try asking for a detox and scrubdown.

All the newly arrived tramps would have been supervised by the wonderfully named Tramp Major. In charge of all aspects of the vagrants' well-being during their stay, the Major would regiment their cleaning, feeding and accommodation. The casuals' food wasn't quite as upmarket as the residents', whose diet of gruel, bread, dripping and potatoes was even supplemented with meat on Sundays and special occasions. Still, the conditions were better in the workhouse than outside and the place became a veritable tramp magnet. Sleeping arrangements were simple – a long corridor of fourteen single night cells, each with a straw bed and a call button, in case the rank-and-file guests wanted to summon the Major in the middle of the night. Admit it, if you had a button labelled 'Tramp Major' next to your bed, the temptation to push it would be unbearable.

The Workhouse Museum does a fantastic job with what it has. Don't expect to be given a guided tour by a robotic Tramp Of The Future and shown interactive computer displays on archaic street fashion. Everything on display has been sourced from the original workhouse, or if an item is unavailable, a local approximation brought in. The two freestanding bathtubs on display are originals reclaimed from the hospital blocks, as are the sinks and the nasty looking restraint chair in one of the cells. The museum is currently waiting for a stone-breaking facility to be transported in and, in an ironic twist, local prisoners have been constructing a sawhorse so the museum can show the tools the casuals would have employed to earn their keep. Items here are acquired as and when they can be afforded. This is solid, no-frills, locally funded history.

The two sister museums to the Tramp Museum (they should rename it, they really should) vary in tone. The Prison and Police Museum on St Marygate is a flashier, lottery-funded affair, with dressing-up boxes full of police helmets and lockable cells with working treadmills and stocks. It has yet another restraining chair and so many varieties of criminal-pounding truncheon that you wonder whether the prisoners would just as easily have been restrained by pouring their pulped remains into a screw-top jar.

The plain-walled Courthouse Museum opposite Ripon Cathedral is more austere altogether, as befits an institution dedicated to no-frills punishment – come up before the beak on a theft charge three times and you would have been clapped in irons and heading for Australia before you knew what hit you.

Ripon's museums are unusual in that they reflect the entire Victorian judicial process. From the mid sixteenth to the late nineteenth century, the city, like many in Britain, had its own self-contained legal system, independent from the rest of the country. This meant that the good people of Ripon were left alone to protect, accuse or punish anyone they fancied. These three museums preserve a unique record of a lost system of law, still housed in the same buildings where that justice would originally have been dealt out.

As with many small attractions, the big question facing this cluster of museums is whether local interest can be sustained to keep them open into the next generation. Bess Chapman, the current curator of the Courthouse Museum, was the magistrate who served the very last session there in 1998 – a fine example of the direct connection local museums can have to the life of the places they serve – but fresh blood is always needed to preserve places such as this.

Perhaps a change of name for the Workhouse Museum might be just the thing to attract an enthusiastic new influx of staff and visitors. Something snappy that catches the eye and makes people want to visit. If only somebody could suggest a good alternative . . .

Llanfairpwllgwyngyllgogery-chwyrndrobwllllan-tysiliogogogoch

I remember your name perfectly; but I just can't think of your face.

Rev. William Archibald Spooner

Until the middle of the nineteenth century, this quiet little village's name was only twenty letters long, and had a space in it. The place pootled along quite happily as Llanfair Pwllgwyngyll (meaning 'St Mary's church near the pool by the white hazels') for centuries, attracting very little attention. The old name did the job perfectly well, being both an adequate descriptive label for the village and impossible to pronounce if you come from anywhere east of Hereford (the secret reason for most Welsh place names).

Then the railways came. The businesses of Llanfair were doubtless excited by the prospect of hundreds of new customers rolling in on the new Chester to Holyhead line. Sadly they noticed that, with no real reason to get off the train at Llanfair, all those travellers' bulging pockets just rolled straight out again, off to somewhere more interesting. An emergency committee was formed to come up with a way to make the passengers literally stop in their tracks.

Which is why Llanfair was rechristened, giving it the longest railway station name in Britain.

As visitors pulled up at the station, the sign hove into view through their carriage window. And kept on heaving. For ages. Humble Llanfair Pwllgwyngyll (the place where nobody got out) was suddenly Llanfairpwllgwyngyllgogerychwyrndrobwllllantysiliogogogoch (the place you simply have to get off the train and look at the sign).

Translated from the Welsh, Llanfair(etc) means

'the church of St Mary in the hollow of the white hazel near the fierce whirlpool and the church of Tysilio by the red cave.' The renaming turned every name board and road sign into a list of (slightly underwhelming) tourist attractions. Perhaps it was hoped that the simple act of listing the attractions in the village's name, like the simple act of posting a menu in the window of a restaurant, would get the punters pouring in. But though the visitors did come, instead of picking a dish off the menu (and going to visit the church, for example) they just stood and looked at the menu a bit more.

They're still doing it today. People arrive. They get off the train or the coach. They stand next to the sign. They don't go and look for the red cave or the fierce whirlpool. They leave. It must have been a revelation to the bright sparks of the committee. People would come just to see the advertising. The brand was everything. The product was nothing. Nike ought to build their HQ here.

The identity of the genius who came up with the idea has sadly now been lost to history, though various claimants have been celebrated in local myth, most notably an unnamed cobbler who lived under the Menai bridge. Ever since Eric the Red hauled his longboat up on some cold and barren landmass and then persuaded gullible Vikings to settle there by calling it Greenland, canny operators have relied on the power of this sort of trick.

Without any actual tourist attractions or particularly unique features, Llanfair PG (as it's officially known) had just decided to make itself sound interesting. Putting up a sign is cheaper and quicker than building a zoo or a castle or waiting for natural forces to carve you a spectacular waterfall. 'That place has got a really excitingly-shaped name,' our stupid brains tell us, 'I bet it's really exciting! Let's go there!'

So it's satisfying to report that, although it's pretty enough, as North Welsh villages go, there is almost nothing of interest in Llanfair at all apart from the name. Once you've seen the station with the very long sign, you can take a little stroll, and maybe visit the wool shop with a very long sign. Make sure you've got plenty of film in your camera, because you won't want to miss the computer repair shop with a very long sign, or the chemist's with its distinctive very long sign. Down the road, heading towards the Britannia Bridge and the mainland, you'll be relieved to hear, there's a Volvo dealership with a very long sign.

Puddles of tourists spill in and out of coaches in

the bustling station car park. They take pictures of each other in front of one or more of the very long signs. They buy a souvenir postcard featuring the very long sign, get it franked with a very long franking stamp, and sit for a while with a cup of tea on a bench (in front of a very long sign), then they move on. Llanfair PG is now firmly part of the tourist trail – to do North Wales and not come here seems like a missed opportunity.

This is tourism stripped to the bare bones. There is no other reason to come here except to take a picture of yourself to prove that you did. It has this in common with places like Wendy in Cambridgeshire – where many a Wendy stops to pose by the roadsign – or otherwise forgotten enclaves like Dull in Perthshire, Titty Hill in Sussex and Britain Bottom in Gloucestershire. The (typically crass) commercial versions are those silly customised finger-posts frequented by beaming Australians so they can go home with a picture of themselves beneath an unfeasible 'Land's End 1, Goondiwindi 10,489.'

There is, actually, something very interesting in Llanfair PG, but it's not advertised in the very long name. Head towards the (unremarkable but pleasant) church of St Mary's by the whirlpool and the red cave of which we have heard so much, and you'll see what looks like Nelson's Column towering over the Menai Strait. The ninety-one foot high monument is topped by the statue of a one-legged man, and commemorates the first Marquess of Anglesey. The Marquess lost his leg fighting alongside Wellington at Waterloo, and insisted the limb be buried on the field of battle with full military honours. He later became the owner of the world's first articulated artificial limb, and got on with it so well he eventually had three different models made – one for riding, one for walking and one for best.

But, of course, no-one makes a journey to Anglesey to see a monument to an artificial leg pioneer. They come here to see the big signs. The baited trap's been working gloriously for 150 years, and we all still fall for it. It's a wonder we do, given that it's far too easy for anyone to do this. If you can be bothered, you can call anywhere whatever you want, let's be honest. It's hardly rocket science.

To prove what an easy trick it is, and with remarkable competitive mean-spiritedness, just down the road, the miniature railway in Gwynedd recently gave its old Golf Halt station a new name nine letters longer than Llanfair's. John Ellerton, owner of the

Fairbourne and Barmouth Steam Railway did it to get into the *Guinness Book of Records*. It worked, and Gorsafawddachaidraigodanheddogleddollonpen-rhynareurdraethceredigion ('the Mawddach station with its dragon's teeth on the northerly Penrhyn drive on the golden beach of Cardigan Bay) now has the longest place name in Britain. We look forward to Llanfair PG upping the ante further by changing its name to Llanfairpwllgwyngyllgogerychwyrndrob-wllllantysiliogogogochaoeddarenwllemwyafhirymm-hrydain ('the church of St Mary in the hollow of the white hazel near the fierce whirlpool and the church of Tysilio by the red cave which used to have the longest place name in Britain').

These two Welsh tourist attractions aren't alone in taking advantage of our fascination with long words. We are very easily dazzled by this sort of thing, even though the words have very often been made up with no other purpose than to impress us. Well-known record breaker pneumonoultramicro-scopicsilicovolcanoconiosis (a lung disease caused by volcanic dust) is actually a fake word, made up by Everett Smith of the American National Puzzlers' League in 1935 for the sheer hell of it, yet it still finds itself in the Webster's, Random House and

Chambers' dictionaries. Like that old schoolroom favourite antidisestablishmentarianism (resistance to the severance of ties between church and state), however, it deserves a place in the dictionary because it's now in surprisingly common usage – because it crops up every time anyone is talking about long words.

It's possible that neither of these monstrous coinages has ever been used in the context of lung trouble or ecclesiastical politics. It's interesting to note that the latter of these two lexical behemoths is now so regularly employed in discussions about long words that the computer spell-check being used for this book had no problem accepting it (although great English words you might use every day such as plimsoll, googly and clanger all get sternly flagged up as questionable – which is why Britain should have worked harder at patenting the computer: see chapter on Bletchley Park).

The Guinness Book of Records makes a distinction between the longest 'real' and the longest 'made up' words, but when you think about it, all words are made up. What we call something is only what we've all agreed to call it. And, thanks to that linguistic loophole, Llanfair has managed to pull off one of tourism's silliest triumphs.

A Victorian wrongasaurus at Crystal Palace

Glass pick 'n' mix.

Dennis Severs' Regency clutter.

Bletchley Park is bursting with the
sort of thing that made Britain great.

A state-of-the-art tramp dip at Ripon.

A llovely llong sign.

South Bridge Vaults: the black hole of Edinburgh.

Honestly, some gnomes have no manners.

A la Ronde: may contain shells.

A village that makes its own sunlight.

Bagpipes trapped safely behind glass.

Bekonscot's tiny town crier.

Hanging out with the stones at Avebury.

The house of the Lord's.

There's an interesting footnote to Llanfair PG's adventures in self-promotion. Having celebrated almost a century and a half as the biggest station name in the world, in October 1999 Llanfair(etc) entered cyberspace by becoming the planet's longest unhyphenated website address. It seems that, as soon as a new technology, whether railways or computers, gives the people of Llanfair a chance to get themselves noticed, they are in there like a shot. The .co.uk version of the village site is full of history and tourist-attracting information, and quite charmingly done, but it gives us great pleasure to report that, at the time of writing, in strict adherence to the spirit of its real life equivalent, if you visit www.llanfairpwllgwyngyll-gogerychwyrndrobwllllantysiliogogogoch.com, there is almost nothing of interest there at all. The Menai cobbler would have been proud.

South Bridge Vaults

Frank stared at the table, hardly daring to stare at the table.

John Lennon, 'Unhappy Frank,' *In His Own Write*

In the world of tourism, is there anything more unseemly, more un-British than the dolling up of a perfectly adequate attraction with unseemly, garish bluster? The heart sinks on discovering that a fondly remembered historic mill has reinvented itself as a Visitor Experience, teeming with drama students in mob caps going 'ooh arr' at school parties. It's undignified, fussy and really Not Quite The Done Thing.

However, judging from the walking tours being offered on display boards up and down the Royal Mile, what the tourists want when they come to Edinburgh is the history of Scotland's capital city, but with the boring school-style facts removed and lots of plastic skellingtons put in. Of all the advertised tours, only a tiny fraction choose not to hawk the city as an extended Chamber of Horrors, practically guaranteeing the agonised spirits of bricked-up urchins screaming every hour on the hour with two matinees on Sundays. It would be easy to blame the Americans. So we will.

In the mind of the average American tourist, anything built before last Thursday simply has to be aching with the restless spirits of the dead. Old Europe can be quite surprisingly old if you've come from a country where the Pirates Of The Caribbean ride at Disneyworld is a national heritage site. So to keep the tours popular with the visitors from the land of All New Everything (and the usual gaggle of slack-minded thrill-seekers from the rest of the world who don't mind learning something as long as it's circumstantial, sensational and attested to by a friend of a friend) some fascinating historical sites are stripped of their intrinsic dignity, their actual past smothered by a load of tosh, all in the interests of keeping the foreign coins flooding in.

So when it comes to guided tours of Edinburgh's odder corners, make your choice carefully. You can be shown something unique and involving and told a little of its history, or you can pay a tenner to be lied to by someone with a torch under their chin.

All of which brings us to Edinburgh's South Bridge Vaults, a haunting, strange, unnerving attraction that doesn't need any urban legends to send a shiver up your spine. Edinburgh has more than its fair share of hidden attractions. The enormous glacial ridge on which it stands has shaped a multilayered city, all slopes and bridges, unexpected drops and streets piled on top of one another. Stroll up Princes Street from Waverley Station, turn right onto the North Bridge and past the Tron along the main road towards the college campus. In a sudden gap between two buildings, another street appears a dizzying distance below you, threaded through the arch of a viaduct on which you had no idea you were standing. This is the South Bridge, and it's hiding from you.

The South Bridge was constructed at the end of the eighteenth century to bring goods and traffic in and out of the booming commercial city. It's as straight as a ruler, an unwavering line drawn across the huge ditch on one side of the glacial escarpment, joining the ridge of the Royal Mile to the hill where the University stands. The bridge is supported by nineteen sets of arches, but rather than leaving the structure open to the air, like most viaducts, the developers erected buildings either side, so that it is mainly concealed from view. Shops on the South Bridge may be two storeys high on the street side, but plunge away a dozen floors further at the rear.

Sealing in the bridge turned its arched cavities into closed chambers. And, business being business, as you might expect, these damp, dark, unpleasant little holes were soon being rented out as storage, work-shop space or even living quarters for the sort of people who really couldn't afford to waste money on expensive luxuries such as light or air.

These eighteenth-century vaults were too badly waterproofed to stay occupied for long, and eventu-ally fell into disuse. They were only rediscovered in the mid-1980s, and a visit retains the sensation of stumbling upon something extraordinary that has always been right under your nose. Walking past nondescript shop backs, the tour guide stops and brandishes a big key. A timid, unmemorable door, peeping shyly between flyposters, is unlocked, creaking open to reveal a flight of steps. Within seconds of stepping inside, you have lost your bearings; it beggars belief that this parallel world could exist woven into a space which already seemed occupied by shops, cafes and pubs.

The journey-to-the-centre-of-the-earth darkness is such that you soon forget that if the buildings were removed either side, the light would flood in and you'd be standing far above the street level, nose-to-beak with the pigeons. The South Bridge Vaults are Britain's premier underground catacomb tour that's actually quite high up in the air.

Though little written evidence exists for what went on here (most business transactions having been conducted on a sticky-sounding 'spit-and-handshake' basis), artefacts found in the vaults have revealed an astonishing breadth of usage – from cobbler's workshops to wine stores – reflecting the fascinating history of the city.

Until 1823, it's interesting to learn, Scotland's national tipple was not whisky, which was outlawed, but claret, imported from France. England was too busy fighting the French to ever stop and ask for a few bottles of their excellent wine, leading to a brisk trade in illegal French booze at the Anglo-Scots border (port travelled in the opposite direction thanks to England's alliances with Spain and Portugal). Any fine claret that wasn't smuggled to thirsty Sassenachs would have been stored and guarded in the gloom of these man-made caves.

And it's the darkness that's so unnerving. The vaults are lit by sparse candles, but this gives a misleading impression of how cosy things might have looked at the time. Bright-burning paraffin wax is a modern invention – a by-product of the petroleum industry developed just in time to be superseded by the lightbulb. And beeswax candles would have been an unimaginable luxury for someone who had chosen to minimise their expenses by living and working in a hole. The only light in these chambers would have come from crude tallow lamps made from smoky, smelly animal fats – effectively butter on fire. This would have been a horrible place to spend what people outside might have distinguished as your 'days' and 'nights'.

There is a whole miniature world in here, though little evidence remains amongst the blank walls and featureless ceilings. One chamber was used as a leather store, another a jewellers – in fact many activities are satisfyingly similar to ones you might expect to find underneath bridge arches today. There's everything apart from a car exhaust repair firm and a lockup containing George Cole and Dennis Waterman. People would work down here without seeing daylight for days. The tour lasts around an hour, and that's unsettling enough.

This is a genuinely strange, affecting place to spend some time, without ever resorting to ghost-train histrionics. But, as so often happens, the paranormal ballyhoo is so important to Edinburgh tourism that it has developed an unstoppable self-sufficient momentum. Search for any newspaper archives or publicity material about the South Bridge Vaults, and you'll soon come across the proud claim that the catacombs' haunted pedigree is such that in 2001 the site was chosen by psychologist Professor Richard Wiseman of the University of Hertfordshire to host the Edinburgh Ghost Project – 'Britain's biggest ever paranormal experiment.' What gets mentioned less often is the study's conclusion. Hold on to your ghost-hunting hats here, this is cutting edge stuff.

Apparently, The Project discovered, if you put lots of people in a cold, nasty room where they can't see properly, assailed by the disorientating subsonic rumble of overhead traffic, and tell them they're taking part in a supernatural experiment, they get all jumpy and uneasy. Then, when they're on edge and confused, they start seeing things in the shadows. Thus the average South Bridge ghost is about as unyielding to rational explanation as the ones in *Scooby Doo*. (A tape of terrifying, muffled 'voices of the dead' recorded in one of the vaults turned out to be people chatting in the massage parlour on the other side of the wall – it's easy to forget in such an eerie place that the world is going about its unctuous business only a few feet away.)

Of course, the big money still rolls in from the spooky ghost tours. Mercat, who organise the excellent history walk round these vaults, run their fair share of chain-rattling events themselves; they're not stupid. But it is disappointing that the folklore is allowed to get in the way of some very interesting history. The atmosphere in these chambers, the sense of an unimaginable shadowy existence lived by ordinary people not so long ago, is haunting enough not to need any ghost stories.

Gnome Magic

It has long been an axiom of mine that the little things are infinitely the most important.

Sir Arthur Conan Doyle, *A Case of Identity*

This is what happens when there isn't a governmental department responsible for maintaining national folklore. Lacking firm guidance from Whitehall, our woodlands are a warring mess of goblins, brownies, piskies and Will o'the Wisps. What we could really do with is a spokesmythological creature. The Irish settled on the leprechaun, the Scandinavians are inexplicably fond of the troll, even the Manx have Arkan Sonney, the lucky piggy. The closest thing we Brits have to a fairy-folk figurehead is the garden gnome. Cheerful, quiet, colourful, adept shoe repairers, gnomes have long been the marketable face of Britain's little people.

They may never have been terribly fashionable but they've remained a stubbornly popular feature in the nation's gardens since 1847 when Sir Charles Isham installed twenty-one terracotta gnomes in the grounds of Lamport Hall, Northamptonshire. The only survivor from this original set is now insured for more than one million pounds, which is a fashionable amount of money at least. None of the 650 static inhabitants of Gnome Magic is yet worth quite this much.

Former printer Michael Bridges had the initial idea for his gentle East Anglian attraction more than a decade ago. After purchasing a property with sufficient garden and woodland space to accommodate his community of concrete gnomes, he sat for a teeth-grinding four years while the council hemmed and hawed about granting him planning permission. This is the result.

A first-time visitor to Gnome Magic can be forgiven for wondering where the gnomes are. A mural in the reception-cum-tea-room depicts Snow White and the Seven Dwarfs. The pedantic might point out that gnomes are dwarfish and that dwarfs aren't gnomish, but before you can even get started on that debate, you're startled by a thirteen-foot high Filipino velociraptor statue staring in through the conservatory window. So far Gnome Magic appears to be fairly gnome-free.

Perhaps it's a security measure. After all, gnome theft has recently seen a sharp increase across Europe. France, home of the Front de Libération des Nains de Jardin (le Garden Gnome Liberation Front) has been hit particularly severely. The ornaments are routinely kidnapped from the lawns of the republic and restored to their natural forest habitat, where they are usually discovered in clusters of about a hundred.

The situation was thought to have been resolved when one of the FLNJ ringleaders was unmasked and convicted of handling stolen gnomes. Not a chance. Eleven gnomes were later discovered under a road bridge at Briey in the northeast of France; they had apparently hanged themselves in a mass suicide. A note left at the scene stated they no longer wished to be 'part of your selfish world, where we serve merely as pretty decoration' and that frankly they were off to a better place.

Gnome Magic's residents, it turns out, have no need to be relocated to a remote glade because they're already in one. The proprietor is obviously one step ahead. Leave the dinosaur, flap yourself a path through the smashing king-sized dragonflies hovering about the garden, and a miniature tree-sheltered world of beards and pipes awaits.

By his own admission, Mr Bridges isn't particularly partial to gnomes. He was once given one as a present and his collection casually grew from there. Hardly any of them have been given names, excepting the benevolent King Gnoman. Instead, Bridges' mental energy appears to have been reserved for dreaming up satirical tableaux in which the gnomes can participate. The Teddy Blair's Picnic and several extremely blunt messages to the Chancellor of the Exchequer concerning the financial well-being of the elderly give the impression that this miniature world has a full-size axe to grind.

Adult visitors would do well to take time to reflect on this form of passive resistance. These solo protests may not be the most effective way of making your dissenting voice heard but imagine if every single garden in Britain had contained a gnome waving a 'NOT IN MY NAME' placard when we were about to invade Iraq. A red-faced Downing Street would have been brought to its knees by the press.

In that event, the Prime Minister might well have cursed August Heissner and Philipp Griebel, two of the most famous names in gnome appreciation circles. In 1875, this enterprising pair oversaw the first mass production of the *erdmanlein*, as Germans call it. Griebel's family still manufacture gentlegnomes and ladygnomes to this day. Thankfully the sexist 'no girls' edict issued by the first, and so far only, International Congress for the Protection of the Garden Gnome (Chemnitz, winter 2002) was ignored by Philipp's grandson Reinhard, who coughed up the 75 euro fine lobbied by the daft congress and ploughed on regardless. The ruling has also been ignored at Gnome Magic, where female gnomes have every right to stand alongside their male counterparts. You can't give in to these people.

Despite not really expressing any great passion for his little concrete charges, Mr Bridges can now proudly claim that Gnome Magic could, in the event of an international shortage, be entirely self-sufficient; he has been on a course to learn how to make gnomes and their moulds. He only does the basic models, mind, and hasn't shown much interest in branching out into the burgeoning market for celebrity garden gnomes. (If you know where to ask, it is now possible to purchase a stone Charlie Dimmock or a fairyland Nicholas Lyndhurst for that gap next to your fishpond, heaven help you.)

Do be aware that gnomes can cause the value of your home to fall as well as stay exactly the same, according to various property experts. This can't be fair. Prospective house buyers should be delighted to see one of these twinkly-eyed toadstool lovers. A gnome suggests that a patch of grass has had genuine care bestowed upon it by the owner. Someone who let their garden go to rack and ruin is hardly likely to make the effort to crown it with a little concrete man.

Gnome Magic offers some timely solutions to its inhabitants' twee reputation. There's square-bashing, a Mr Universe competition, seemingly blissed-out hippie gnomes, and an uninvestigated murder scene. Where are the gnome police when you need them? Hiding from those incongruous clown figures probably. Or up in the trees. Tall people and those with big hats beware.

We all occasionally desire a taste of the fantastic, and a meeting with these Essex homunculi – be they a flowerpot-hatted regiment of gardeners with little trowels or a horde of miniature naturists sunning themselves by the pond – is a fetching alternative to watching endless deleted scenes from *Lord of the Rings* if you want to get your fill of small people.

A la Ronde

We are a nation of flower-lovers, but also a nation of
stamp-collectors, pigeon-fanciers, amateur carpenters,
coupon-snippers, darts-players, crossword-puzzle fans.
It is the liberty to have a home of your own, to do
what you like in your spare time, to choose your own
amusements instead of having them chosen for you
from above.

George Orwell, *The Lion and The Unicorn*

At the end of the eighteenth century, two spinster
cousins, Jane and Mary Parminter, planned,
realised and decorated what must be one of Britain's

most unusual residences. Down a quiet lane over-looking the splendid expanse of the Exe valley, their bizarre home stands as a shrine to what can be achieved away from the distractions of marriage.

A la Ronde is completely off-the-radar. Packed to the rafters with the accumulated detritus of decades of spinsterish handicraft – découpage, shellwork, feather displays – this is what happens when sensible rainy day hobbies are allowed to run unchecked. It's also a very unusual shape. Based around a central octagonal reception hall, the building is effectively hexadecagonal, which, before you consult your trusty *I-Spy Book Of Big Shapes*, means it has sixteen sides. What's more, you enter the house on the first floor (although it's really the ground floor) and leave from the basement, with your brain on inside out.

The head-spinning geometry of A la Ronde might be more easily understood if we knew a little more about its creators. Unfortunately information about the Parminters has been scant ever since the family documents were moved to the records office in Exeter where the Luftwaffe could destroy them more easily during the bombing of the city in April 1942. We do know that Jane's father, John, was a businessman from Barnstaple who had successfully embraced

European trade by opening a wine exporters in Lisbon. Unfortunately when an earthquake devastated the Portuguese capital in November 1755, it ruined not only his booze business but also everything else around it, killing tens of thousands of people.

This tragedy fired Mr Parminter's brain into overdrive. He sensibly decided that, although it might have temporarily helped to dull the city's collective pain, wine wasn't what Lisbon needed most right now. No, what the city needed was quick-drying cement. Lots of it and quickly. So he began to manufacture masses of the stuff. King Joseph of Portugal was so impressed by this display of enterprising generosity that he had a glass factory built for Mr Parminter as a reward. The mental leap which King Joseph was making from wine to cement to glass manufacturing is one seldom attempted, but perhaps he was dropping a subtle hint that his new, rapidly drying buildings needed some windows.

Wherever their wealth sprang from, there's no doubt that by the latter half of the eighteenth century, the Parminters were minted. How else could they have afforded in 1784 to send the two spinster cousins, Jane's invalid sister Elizabeth and a friend on an inspirational (and unusually for the time, ladies-only) eleven-year knees-up round Europe?

We can only assume that Mr Parminter funded the trip out of compassion for the tragic individuals involved. His daughter, Jane, was 34 and still single, 17-year-old Mary had been an orphan since the age of 12, and Elizabeth was a sickly 28-year-old. The cultural jaunt proved a marvellous tonic for the group and was a great influence on their later life, excepting Elizabeth who keeled over and died on their return in 1795. Undeterred, the cousins decided that the journey had been such a blinder that they would have a house built in Exmouth which they could decorate with the spoils of their travels.

Precisely who built A la Ronde remains a mystery. Because the building is such a one-off it is not easy to trace the architect through their style. Several names have been put forward, but since the house plans were blitzed with the rest of the family's records, short of finding a signed confession some-where, we'll never know for sure. Suffice to say that whoever built such a property must have known the eccentric cousins very well indeed.

'Eccentric', meaning literally 'out of centre' or 'deviating from a circular path' is a good word for describing the ladies and their silly house. The Parminters retreated into a little world of their own at A la Ronde – even having a chapel put up in the grounds because they'd got tired of walking to the one in Exmouth. They then erected a school and some almshouses, and started writing peculiar wills.

In Jane's she stated that the school be run purely for the education of girls and that the almshouses should ideally be reserved for Jewish spinsters who had decided to convert to Christianity. Not wanting to be outdone and with the stubborn illogic of some-body who'd spent half a century living in a thatched chocolate box, Mary's will specified that the house and contents were only to be passed down through the unmarried women of the family.

Since the owners were two ageing spinster cousins, the odds of A la Ronde ever being inherited seemed slim. However, Jane's two unmarried second cousins, Jane and Sophia Hurlock, fitted the bill and took on the house after Mary's death in 1849. Next up on the unmarry-go-round was the Hurlocks' niece Stella who, after inheriting the property, managed to break with convention and tie the knot. Via a loophole in property law she bypassed the 'single female' stipu-lation and handed the place on to her brother, the

Reverend Oswald Reichel, who, unless he had a secret under his cassock, was really bending the rules.

A la Ronde was by now, thanks to generations of spinsters, a riot of industrious feminine handicraft, and Reichel found himself compelled to stamp a clodhopping manly footprint on it, performing all manner of naughty Victorian DIY. He installed a terrifying central heating system made from huge, black pipes; replaced the thatch with tiles; knocked down interior walls; and put in a dumb waiter. More changes occurred after Reichel's death when the house passed back to yet further spinster ownership. Somehow the owners managed to convert it into four private flats before the National Trust stepped in and took over the property in 1991. Since then the house has been preserved in a state of well-kept equilibrium, with much of the original decor restored. Any necessary additions are unobtrusive, including an environmentally friendly heating system whose custom-made radiators shame Reichel's overbearing monster plumbing nicely.

The shape of the house, probably influenced by Jane and Mary's memories of the octagonal tower on the church of San Vitale in Ravenna, is both decorative and practical. The sixteen sides make the building particularly stable (the Normans knew what they were doing with their round towers) whilst providing the women with an all day suntrap, taking full advantage of the random dribbles of sunlight the British climate coughs up when it can be bothered. The morning sun would shine into the two east-facing bedrooms (now the study and music room) and gradually follow the cousins round the house until it set in the west-facing dining room at the end of the day.

The octagonal central hall sets a geometric precedent which continues around the house from chairs to tables to mirrors (a pentagonal loft hatch breaks with the theme a little, but it's still one side more than you'll find in most properties). Suspended centrally from the ceiling is an ornamental dove carrying a silver globe (which mirrors the entire room from any angle). This apparatus is said to have been used by the cousins to spy on visitors. Its resemblance to a 'gazing' or 'witch' ball is worth noting, especially in the Exmouth/Topsham area where superstitious locals believed that the hundred mile long track of hoofprints they found in the snowfall one night in February 1855 were caused by the Devil. A house this skewed would have been a magnet for someone who walked backwards.

Similar geometric games are played around the rest of the property. Alternate square sash and diamond casement windows circle the house on the vertices of its sixteen sides. This means that each window bows outward in the middle at 157½ degrees. Whilst the witch ball may have repelled the Devil himself, such showboating craftsmanship would certainly have seen off even the most persistent of his double-glazing selling acolytes.

Moving between the study and music room, the more eagle-eyed visitor may spot a seashell or two, with further conchology evident in the library where a cabinet full of pipes, stones and trinkets also has a fine selection of shells on display. Keep these in mind as you pass through the bedroom with its shell lampshade and the room containing Mrs Mellows' shell collection on your way to the Shell Staircase leading to the Shell Gallery and appreciate the daily three-hour cleaning headache facing the National Trust staff. Suddenly every corner of the property (and there are a lot of them) appears to be filling with shells.

Perched atop A la Ronde like a jaunty crustaceous crown, the Shell Gallery stands as a fine example of why retiring children should be encouraged to go outside more often. Obviously the result of one too many days spent in isolation, these rooms are simultaneously the Parminter cousins' most spectacular and most frightening achievement. Though both the Staircase and Gallery are now far too delicate to allow visitors in, those foolhardy enough to want to bear witness to its molluscan majesty can get their carapacious kicks via an ingenious closed circuit camera set up (joystick included) by the tea rooms. Bet you weren't expecting that.

From here on in the decoration simply doesn't let up. The drawing room's feather coving took the cousins seventeen years to create. The Parminters' original fireplace on the eastern wall is filled with and surrounded by yet more shells, with plenty of shells on the mantelpiece for good measure. An octagonal table, surrounded by three octagonal chairs bears the weight of an octagonal tray decorated in seaweed. Surrounded by such ornament, ironically the Reverend Reichel's plain wooden fireplace provides blessed relief to the eye.

A la Ronde is a delightful exercise in Victorian decorative excess – dolls' house taste run riot. Now the over-dressing is the careful responsibility of the National Trust, the mind boggles with thoughts of how much more intricately cluttered it must have looked by the time the Parminter cousins left – after all some of the decoration is bound to have been lost to successive ownership and the need for living space. As you leave through the downstairs tea rooms (where a cream tea is highly recommended), take a second to check out the goose-cote in the garden by the car park. It's a small, octagonal (naturally) affair with red rimmed diamond windows around the sides and a tiny fake cupola. And, likely as not, it's home to two spinster geese who are slowly filling it with goose feathers and goose shells for the lack of anything else to do.

Port Sunlight

Cash payment is not the only nexus between man and man.

William Ewart Gladstone, speech at Port Sunlight

Utopians are, by nature, a funny lot. Edward Craven Walker, who dreamed of a better world where nobody wore any clothes, invented the lava lamp after staring for rather too long at an egg timer in a pub. Charles Fourier, the Utopian Socialist, predicted that the Arctic Ocean was one day going to lose its salt and turn into a kind of lemonade. William Hesketh Lever, the Victorian soap tycoon and worker-relations idealist, slept outside on the roof.

Philanthropic Utopians often like to splash their spare oof about creating spectacular architectural legacies. Dame Henrietta Barnett left us Hampstead Garden Suburb (with its twittens and open-air theatre), Titus Salt built Saltaire (including atop one of its wool mills a prize to himself – the biggest room in the world) and William Hesketh Lever created the lemony fresh village of Port Sunlight.

If you're not immediately familiar with the name, William Hesketh was the Lever of Unilever, the commercial behemoth responsible for an exhausting number of brands including Marmite, Magnum, Domestos, Dove, Hellmann's, Colman's, Bird's Eye, Ben & Jerry's, Carte D'Or, Vaseline, Chicken Tonight, Cerruti 1881, Lux, Lynx, Lipton, PG Tips, Pot Noodle, Persil, Bertolli, Mentadent, Timotei, Ambrosia, Impulse, SlimFast, Cif (née Jif), cK one, Flora, Knorr and Comfort Easy Iron (which was invented in Port Sunlight). In other words, to paraphrase Sir Christopher Wren's epitaph in St Paul's Cathedral, if you seek his monument, look in your cupboards.

But Port Sunlight is a far more striking legacy even than Comfort Easy Iron. Lever made his fortune manufacturing Sunlight soap ('So Clean'), and this absurdly pretty enclave is perhaps the only place in the country to be named after a product.* This has, mercifully in most cases, never caught on: the suggestion to raise money for London Underground by selling off tube station names to corporate sponsors has been pooh-poohed more than once, saving passengers from such rot as Red Leicester Square, Branston Piccadilly Circus and eBayswater.

William Lever grew up in Bolton, a city which the Industrial Revolution had made overcrowded and filthy and successful – the common contradiction of a wealthy boomtown where people lived and worked in disgusting squalor. The sight of all this bustling filth made a big impression on the young man. At the age of sixteen, he joined his father's wholesale business as an apprentice, cutting and wrapping soap. Two decades later, he was still cutting and wrapping soap, but 14,000 tons of it a week from his Lever Bros works in Warrington.

*Cadbury's Bournville chocolate was named after the suburb where their Victorian factory stood, not vice versa. Similarly the planet Mars had been around a fair length of time before someone thought of immortalizing it in cocoa.

Lever, like any successful industrialist, wanted to build the most state-of-the-art factory possible, thus maximising output of his bestselling product – a winning combination of boiled tallow, cotton oil, pine resin, coconut palm kernels and citronella (so that's why it tastes like that). But Lever was a fervent philanthropist, and wealth played on his mind. He said of his whopping profits, '£50,000 a year. Whose is that money? For I want to give it to the man that ought to have it.'

His solution was to buy a messy, marshy acreage on the south bank of the River Mersey and build Port Sunlight, a place where his employees could work, live and – most crucially – improve themselves. Unlike the unforgiving, soot-caked back-to-backs which housed most of Britain's factory workers, the poky holes that fifty years later were making George Orwell chew his moustache in Socialist indignation, Lever's new staff houses had front and back gardens, and were let at reduced rents. But it didn't stop there. There were schools, allotments, a library, an art gallery, a gymnasium, a technical college, an open-air swimming pool, a village hall, bowling greens, a railway station, a post office, a bank, a church, an hotel and a home for Lever and his family – complete with the required outdoor bedroom. These days, you're lucky if your job comes with a handful of luncheon vouchers.

Visiting Port Sunlight today, you can't help but think of Lever's slogan – it really is 'So Clean'. You've never seen so little litter in your life. It's actually quite alarming. Faced with spotless street after spotless street, you start to feel uneasy, that some invisible army of aproned dailies is waiting in the hedges for you to pass, ready to leap out and pick up any loose dust you've kicked up.

In many ways, Lever's vision was directly opposite to, say, that of Prince Charles. Poundbury, the Prince's egregious architectural Utopia in Dorset, is a re-creation of something that never was, a Britain that only exists in His Royal Head. By harking back to a fantasy past and implying the future will be simply ghastly, it inspires very little affection and optimism – and rather too much dreary argument about the merits of different architectural styles. Bollocks to it. Port Sunlight succeeds exactly where Poundbury fails, because it's an upbeat vision of what Britain could be, rather than a proscriptive vision of what it should be or a dewy-eyed ersatz version of what it used to be.

The big thing in Port Sunlight, though – the thing there's more of than anything else – is space. There are open vistas everywhere: greens, avenues, copses, gardens, gaps, paths, terraces, monuments. The pavements are twelve feet wide; the roads three times that. Planning regulations of the time permitted a maximum of forty-two houses to be built on one acre of land: Port Sunlight never has more than seven.

On a good day, Port Sunlight is more than worthy of its name, light pouring in through its thousands of unconventionally-shaped windows. The houses, the work of a clutch of architects led by William Owen and including the young Edwin Lutyens are singularly unpredictable, by turns unusual, funky, curlicued, colourful, pretty, bold and bonkers. Because it isn't shackled by the slavish conservatism of somewhere like Poundbury, there are flashes of wit and impossibility: tudor homes terraced against stone workers' cottages, landlocked seafront villas, crescents of gingerbread houses with heart-shaped holes cut in the shutters, Gormenghast mansions, buildings with cylindrical and conical porches or pargeting on the front and red bricks on the back. Any photographer worth his salt could spend a few hours here and come away with a lifetime's portfolio of biscuit tin lid and jigsaw commissions.

Everywhere you look, Port Sunlight is bubbling with colour. Heaven knows how many hundreds of thousands of flowers there are, neatly pruned and deadheaded, showering the village in a carnival of pinks, yellows and reds. Ageing postcards lead you to believe that Britain used to be saturated in garish Technicolor hues: here it still is. This is how Sir John Betjeman would have seen the world if he'd ever experimented with LSD.

Which brings us neatly to the Beatles. You can't move in or around Liverpool without treading in mop-top droppings, and Port Sunlight is no exception. For it was here, in the Hulme Hall (originally a girls' dining room) on Saturday 18 August, 1962 that John, Paul and George took to the stage with a local lad called Ringo, who was sitting in for a bed-ridden Pete Best. That'll be the birth of the Greatest Group The World Will Ever Know, then. Yet not a blue plaque or a graffito in sight . . .

Lever and his wife ran Port Sunlight like a prototype commune, but with Macassar oil in its hair rather than flowers. He encouraged sobriety (the magnificent Bridge Inn pub was originally a temperance hotel) and insisted upon good workmanship and even better citizenship from his charges: failing at either would strip you of both job and home. That said, Lever was no high-handed dictator, and treated his workforce as human beings rather than easily replaceable components in a moneymaking machine. Indeed, he seems to have been no fan of money at all. He despised bankers (a sign of an essentially sound mind) and wasn't afraid to give his white collar staff a good ticking-off if they abused their expense account – abuse being defined as sharing a cab with fewer than about half a dozen other members of senior management in a pile.

Lever steered his business from strength to strength and continued tinkering with Port Sunlight to the end. The swimming pool and gymnasium are now gone, along with a perfect replica of Shakespeare's house. Viscount Leverhulme, as he later became, flirted with vegetarianism and gymnastics, lectured his workforce on the benefits of chewing each mouthful of food at least thirty-two times, and had himself an uncommonly high desk built so he could work standing up. In fact, the man who slept on the roof and took near-freezing baths did only one truly, saw-it-coming-a-mile-off, utterly predictable thing in his entire life when, in 1925, he died of pneumonia.

There's a tremendous amount to see at Port Sunlight, even if you're just ambling along Jubilee Crescent or taking the air in Greendale Road. Every building, from the Lady Lever Art Gallery (a giant oyster in Portland stone) down to the most modest kitchen cottage, has some twist or trick. Betjeman could have told a volute from a mullion, even if he had been tripping his laureate tits off, but you don't have to be an architectural historian to enjoy Port Sunlight, because it's done with such imagination and wit that your face starts to ache from smiling.

But leaving the village, from any of its exits, is – without exaggeration – an enormous shock. It's like crashing from Oz back to Kansas; everything seems to drain of colour. The grey, tubular bus stop round the corner from Aldi might as well have been reclaimed from Checkpoint Charlie. You half expect the clouds to gather and urine to start falling from the sky. And yet, the area around Port Sunlight is not especially unpleasant, unwelcoming, untidy or unloved. It's just the same as ninety per cent of Great Britain: pretty bloody ordinary. But you've just stepped out of somewhere so pleasant, so welcoming,

So Clean and so adored that anything short of Machu Picchu would be a crushing disappointment. Port Sunlight does exactly what it was intended to do for its workers – it raises the expectations.

Morpeth Bagpipe Museum

The train stopped with a hiss. Everything was quiet.
Then from the far end of the platform came a sound
. . . a musical sound.

'The pipes!' whispered Dougal. 'Oh, the pipes! I may
cry!'

Eric Thompson, *Dougal's Scottish Holiday*

At the top of the list of instruments that parents dread their children taking up, above the drum kit and the alpine horn, is the bagpipe. Bagpipes are the Marmite of the musical world. You either love them or hate them. And, bang in the heart of Northumbrian pipe country is Britain's foremost collection of this controversial instrument. Dozens of them, splayed against their glass cases like tartan spiders.

Housed in a picturesque thirteenth-century stone chantry chapel by a bridge over the River Wansbeck, this is one of Britain's prettier museums, putting the usual Nissen-hut-full-of-pots firmly in the shade. One of only five bridge chantries in existence in Britain, the building was originally constructed as a chapel and grammar school. The adjacent bridge was built around the same time, with the chapel carefully placed in just the right position to act as a tollbooth. Never ones to miss a trick, the Church.

Although you can still see parts of it, the old bridge was demolished in 1829 to make way for a more stable replacement. The Chantry, however, remained and, over the following years, saw service in a number of guises, being used variously, though thankfully not simultaneously, as a mineral water factory, public conveniences, café and cholera hospital.

Restored to its former glory in the 1980s, the Chantry's function remains as manifold and confusing as ever. It now has three jobs, containing not only the Morpeth tourist information centre but also a Northumbrian Craft Shop and, of course, the Bagpipe Museum.

Bagpipes have been with us since Roman times, and may date from even earlier. The principle is simple: what would happen if you crossed an oboe with a lung? The bag (the lung) provides the air supply to sound the chanter (the oboe). Out comes a sound. Everyone starts dancing or marching. The construction is so straightforward that our ever-inventive mediaeval ancestors were known to make a rudimentary version by sticking a whittled pipe and chanter through the hollowed-out corpse of a whole pig.

The man responsible for the collection of pipes and piping paraphernalia now held at Morpeth, William Alfred Cocks, born in Ryton, County Durham, was a clockmaker by trade. During the 1914–18 war, Cocks, possibly frustrated at the lack of noise that his clocks were making, started collecting bagpipes. He was so taken with the instrument that he also began playing and manufacturing his own pipes and was later fundamental in the setting up of the Northumbrian Pipers' Society.

On Cocks' death in 1971 his collection was bequeathed to the Society of Antiquaries in Newcastle who, for over a decade, displayed the bagpipes in a small museum in the town's Black Gate. The damp castle keep wasn't the ideal place to store the delicate instruments and the collection was moved in the 1980s to the then recently restored Chantry in Morpeth, where they were placed safely behind glass for you to enjoy today.

Passing the rack of bagpipe CDs for sale (featuring such timeless classics as *Billy Pigg: The Border Minstrel*) the first thing to strike you as you come off the stairs is the museum's size. It's tiny. The bagpipes themselves take up only one of the Chantry's two upper rooms and the second is used to display a small history of the collection and local piping. If you were expecting the entire building to be crammed to the beams with musettes, zampognas and dudelsacks, you may well be disappointed.

The braver visitor can pick up a set of wireless headphones which brings each exhibit wheezing and coughing to noisy life as you pass its cabinet, like a mediaeval Rock Circus. This system works well unless you stop momentarily between two display cases, when it sounds as if you're earwigging a kazoo-eating competition on a police radio channel.

The museum's local speciality is the Northumbrian Pipes. The last surviving English bagpipes, these instruments differ from their more famous Scottish McCousin in that their air supply is drawn from bellows held under the arm rather than blown in from the mouth, so they can be comfortably played without the musician turning purple. Local belief holds that Northumbrian pipes suit an intimate, indoor environment, while Scottish pipes are best heard outdoors. (Ideally, many would say, from two or three hundred miles away, in a soundproofed concrete underground bunker, with your head placed under a big pile of cushions.)

We make a return to Marmite. You either like pipes, or you don't. Even amongst fans, there are those who adore certain pipes and can't stand others. Perhaps even these sub-groups divide further and further into fiercely polarised breakaway factions, with strong preferences for individual finger holes.

A cursory glance through the museum's visitors' book proves this point. Reactions range from the genuinely surprised ('first bagpipe museum I've ever seen') to the genuinely confused ('we thought it was OK but there should be another room for baller-inas'). There's also room in the book for the more judgmental to express their views. One young visitor warns that 'it was very good and some music was boring,' whilst another opines, 'it is fablus I don't like the Scotchman.'

However, some people, it seems, are just plain furious. 'Je n'aime pas les cornemuses' shouts Irate of Bordeaux from one of the later pages. (No prizes for guessing what *cornemuses* are.) This poor gentleman has worked himself into such a Gallic lather about cornemuses that he's scrawled the same message diagonally across the following page too, with the 'n'aime pas' part heavily underlined. At least the little girl who didn't like the Scotchman put a smiley face and a balloon heart next to her comment.

Of course, this collection isn't here just to annoy the French. Far from being solely a collection of historical pipes, the museum is a living celebration of the instrument. A notice on one of the doorposts reveals that the museum's music and dancing licence has recently been renewed. The Northumbrian Pipers' Society meet here twice a month – a suitably mediaeval playing venue, safely away from furious Frenchmen and ballerina enthusiasts.

Though everything about this tiny museum feels right, there's trouble brewing beneath the surface. Given the Chantry's regular changes of use and the nomadic past of the bagpipe collection, it was bound to happen at some point. It looks as if Mr Cocks' pipes are set to be rehoused again.

At the time of writing, there are plans to maximise the building's tourism potential. Admission charges were removed in April 2003 in an attempt to attract more visitors. However, the increase wasn't significant enough for Castle Morpeth Council who, concerned with the cost of overheads, are seeking an alternative venue.

One of the suggested solutions is to rehouse the collection within one of the county's other tourist attractions, which would be a shame, because this combination of beautiful building and wilfully unusual museum is rather pleasant, certainly more so than putting the bagpipes in a zoo or on board a rollercoaster. If the pipes and craft shop do move, the prospect of the Chantry being turned into a medieval theme bar and grill looms ever closer.

Unfortunately, the small size of the collection makes the whole museum extremely easy to relocate. There are no enormous dinosaur skeletons to pull down and reassemble, no large numbers of indistinguishable flints to shift, and the walls don't need to be carefully stripped of Old Masters – which is a pity because Morpeth Bagpipe Museum seems to work so well where it is. The beauty of this collection comes from its size, subject and setting. And the Scotchman, of course.

Bekonscot

Time goes, you say? Ah no!
Alas, Time stays, we go.
Henry Austin Dobson, *The Paradox of Time*

Just over three-quarters of a century ago, a Bucking-hamshire accountant was standing in his garden, staring at the huge, ugly mound of earth he'd made while digging a pond, and wondering what to do with all that soil before his wife saw it. Indoors, his wife was just about to pop out and have a word about how his model-making obsession was cluttering up their smart Beaconsfield home. With admirable

343

spouse-placating skills, Roland Callingham killed two model birds with one model stone by landscaping the earth around his pond and sticking his collection of little buildings on top. A friend, James Shilcock, impressed by what he saw, donated a model railway to weave through the model houses. Callingham, from Beaconsfield, and Shilcock, from Ascot, christened their new project Bekonscot.

Bekonscot, with the help of Callingham's head gardener and several willing local volunteers, soon evolved into the world's very first model village – described by an advertising pamphlet of the time as 'a modern fairyland'. As the railway track lengthened, so the village grew until it became the sprawling miniature county around which the trains meander today – from the gay fairground at Evenlode, via the art deco aerodrome at Splashyng, to the castle ruins opposite Epwood racecourse.

The village was a huge hit, and even won royal approval from Queen Mary, who became a regular visitor. You can see why she liked it. A stroll round this glorious little corner of Little England is like munching on a cream-smothered slice of pre-war Home Counties flavoured cake. This is the same version of England that, although it never really existed, haunts the dreams of Conservative politicians and local newspaper letters page correspondents – a vision of a nation before some unspecified fall from grace, before the traffic wardens, the media studies lecturers, the new age travellers and the lesbians took over.

But the village hasn't always been like this. For many years, the curators of Bekonscot felt compelled to move with the times, the miniature local council merrily following the example of town planners all over the normal-sized country. Concrete buildings gradually replaced those of historic interest. Railway stations at Maryloo and Greenhaily were updated several times, shunting their steam trains off to the sidings, filling the tramsheds with blue and yellow diesel engines, even replacing their elaborate Edwardian platform canopies with the same unattractive concrete slab roofs that were being inflicted on commuters in the big world.

However, in 1992, in a fit of nostalgia that much of middle England and the proprietor of the *Daily Mail* might wish could be repeated on a much larger scale, Year Zero was declared. The village was restored to its early 1930s glory, eradicating just about any trace of the difficult decades since Bekonscot was born. Grey 1960s office blocks were torn down and mock Tudor pargeted cottages sprang up in their place. Flat-topped bus stations and thin-handed factory clocktowers tumbled as an idealised version of how Buckinghamshire had probably never been was erected instead. This ruthless historical revisionism meant that the fallout from the poll tax riots, the Sex Pistols and the end of Empire need never trouble the oblivious statuettes again. Amongst the pretty villages, picturesque fishing ports and quaint market towns there is even a thriving mining community who remain forever untouched by the efficiency drives of the National Coal Board.

Wandering round you'll see a tiny blacksmith shoeing a tiny horse belonging to a tiny travelling tinker. You can't move without tripping over a shin-high thatched cottage or a pint-sized gymkhana. Time stands absolutely still in every sense, to the extent that the church choir stubbornly continue bellowing out Christmas carols even though it's the middle of July. If this all sounds a touch Enid Blyton-esque then it's no coincidence. The undisputed mistress of picnic descriptions lived just down the road for some thirty years and even wrote *The Enchanted*

Village, a short story about Bekonscot, because she loved it so terribly much.

Blyton's Beaconsfield residence, Greenhedges, was demolished several years ago, but still survives here in model form. The keen-eyed may spot everyone's favourite rosy-cheeked cabbie Noddy parked on her driveway. This is one of the very rare moments when the attraction bothers to pay lip service to anything as vulgar as popular culture. Kids might think that they've spotted a diminutive builder with a mild air of Bobishness about him; closer inspection reveals that he is merely a model villager who just happens to share Bob's taste in orange-and-yellow checked shirts. Yes, there is a Volkswagen Beetle in the garage with Herbie's racing number, but it's probably just a coincidence. Surely the citizens of Bekonscot would never stand for that sort of unseemly branding. Apart, of course, from the perfectly named Ovaltine Farm.

Because it's an outdoor attraction in 1:12 scale, there's much entertainment to be had when the real and the small clash. Rowers on Bekonscot's lake remain steely and focused in the finest Oxbridge tradition, unfazed by the enormous koi carp that casually swim, shark-like, beneath their boats. A crow lands on a village green and you half expect it to drag a fibreglass morris dancer screaming into the air like something from a Ray Harryhausen film, but the dancers wassail on.

For understandable reasons of space, the railway is at 1:32 scale – three times smaller than the rest of Bekonscot – meaning all sorts of humane transporting regulations would be infringed should any of the six-inch-high commuters attempt to squash themselves into the tiny carriages. Instead they wait patiently on the many platforms, hoping one day that the rail companies will send some bigger rolling stock.

Almost a quarter of a mile of miniature track is laced through the grounds, used by up to a dozen different locomotives, all operated from a magnificently restored full-size signal box. Peer through the window and you'll glimpse a magical lost world of twinkling lights and gleaming levers that wouldn't have looked out of place in the days before Dr Beeching took his hefty sledgehammer to the nation's rail network.

The entirety of Bekonscot can be seen from almost wherever you stand but it isn't easy to drag your

attention away from whichever section you're currently Gullivering above, so dense is the level of
detail. Thankfully a viewing platform is handily provided halfway along the path around the village.
Looking down from on high, you can see all the
carefully tended shrubs pretending to be trees. It's a
reminder that you are actually standing in what used
to be someone's private garden.

Bekonscot's architect Roland Callingham died
more than fifty years ago, so the inhabitants of his
tiny world could probably be forgiven for failing to
remember him. However, as with all decent God-
fearing communities, they have sensibly chosen to
honour their Great Creator. His beatific image is
painted on the sign hanging outside the Earl of
Bekonscot pub from where he looks down tolerantly
on drinkers. An obelisk dedicated to him is situated
right next to the exit and stands several feet high
(effectively several miles high if you're a resident).

Callingham's masterpiece was so successful that it
immediately inspired imitators. In 1935, Cotswold
innkeeper Mr Morris (a man from an era where
forenames were unnecessary) was so impressed with
Callingham's triumph that he transformed his own
vegetable garden into a replica of the village in which

he lived; the absurdly picturesque Bourton-on-the-Water in Gloucestershire. Every building in the model was carved in authentic Cotswold stone, including the problematic feature of a model of the model village itself in Morris' model garden (which in turn includes a model of the model, and so on, which will delight anyone interested in fractal mathematics).

When the time comes to leave Bekonscot, a sign points back to the start. Some of the younger visitors will need no prompting to toddle round again for a final farewell. They'll wave a poignant goodbye to all of their new best friends – perhaps the slightly scary netball players, greengrocer Chris P. Lettis or the confused firemen who can't seem to put out the real, smoking house fire no matter how much effort they've put into it over the past seventy-five years.

Other model villages around the country struggle to attract tourists and unhappily they appear to be a dying breed. Southport, part of the mighty Dobbins Brothers model village empire (along with those at Great Yarmouth and Babbacombe) was sold in 1979 and eventually demolished – ironically by rather small bulldozers – to make way for a typically monstrous supermarket. Bekonscot is not only the first but the finest such folly. It deserves to be celebrated as a stubbornly nostalgic monument to Britain's rose-tinted relationship with its own past.

Avebury Stone Circle

Antiquities are history defaced, or some remnants of history which have casually escaped the shipwreck of time.

Francis Bacon, *The Advancement of Learning*

If you're travelling down to Wiltshire in search of ancient monuments, one of the best pieces of advice you could be given is to give Salisbury Plain a miss and head towards Avebury. That way you can enjoy one of the nation's great days out: Not Going To Stonehenge. Because if there is a tourist attraction that qualifies as a national disgrace, something handled so badly that it forms an ugly scar on the face of Britain, it's Stonehenge.

For Britons, stone circles are a vital link with the prehistory of our islands. Without them we'd have no idea what our ancestors were up to before Roman and French invaders started insisting we write it all down. And, despite the hordes of well-meaning hippies who've claimed these ancient stones as their own, you don't have to believe in ley lines or be dressed as a druid to get tingles up your spine at a Neolithic monument.

It doesn't matter whether these things were spiritual batteries, calendars, temples or Britain's earliest fish-and-chip shops, whatever they were, your great great great great great grandparents cared about them enough to use every ounce of their willpower and ingenuity to move lots of enormous stones into important-looking shapes. That's an incredible thought. If you can get a kick out of the sheer force of will it must have taken to build York Minster, you can get a kick out of a stone circle.

These monuments express mankind's relationship to our environment, staking a place out between the earth and the sky (and whatever the builders thought might be beyond), which makes what has been done to Stonehenge a national and historical insult.

Trapped in the crook of two A-roads, ringed with wire fencing, approached through a turnstile and a concrete underpass, strangled by queues of people stuffing their faces with food bought from what looks like a huddle of motorway burger vans at the entrance, our most famous stone circle has been robbed of its every last scrap of awe and splendour. It has all the sad, compromised dignity of a lion in a cage at a regional zoo.

Visiting Stonehenge is no longer a way to plunge yourself neck-deep into the atmosphere of Britain's ancient past, it's a way to insulate yourself against it with cagoules and souvenirs, cement and chicken-wire. You have more chance of a shivery prehistoric epiphany going to see the plastic version at Legoland, and the queue's probably shorter.

The sheer fame of Stonehenge has meant that visitors and passers-by need to be shepherded and corralled, kept apart from the henge itself, thus ensuring they will never experience it as the makers intended; as something to be approached and seen, felt and touched. It's depressing to think that this circle has been here for 4,000 years, but, from the look of the security measures, we belong to the first few generations who apparently can't be trusted not to knock it over or carve our names into it.

Stonehenge has fallen over before, of course – it was only fully reconstructed in the 1920s, shored up with cement and new foundations. People had leant on it and taken bits home as souvenirs for centuries until it was fenced in around a hundred years ago (to a chorus of local disapproval, possibly over the exorbitant shilling admission charged by the then landowners). A widely published photograph shows that people were quite free to paint the word 'Elvis' on the side as recently as 1959. It survived all that all right. It's a terrible shame that it suddenly needs to be so cosseted. It's meant to be part of the landscape, not a delicate ornament. Surely its makers intended that people would interact with the thing, not be kept at a distance.

The argument could of course be made that if you treat people like untrustworthy children, they start behaving like untrustworthy children, and that without all the turnstiles and barricades, and with a bit of common sense, Stonehenge would survive for the next four thousand years as well as it has ever done. The proof of this is only a few miles down the road, where Avebury's stone circle has been left out in the fields for people to play with. They've bashed holes in it, mucked about with it and sat on it for hundreds of years longer than its neighbour. And it knocks Stonehenge into a cocked coracle.

Encouraging King Charles II to pop down for a day trip, the seventeenth-century historian and antiquary John Aubrey described Avebury as a cathedral compared with Stonehenge's parish church. The current situation, Avebury quiet and largely passed over, Stonehenge heaving with backpacks, is as ludicrous as if tourists were pouring into Venice, and rushing past St Peter's Basilica to have a look at a prefabricated boat hut round the corner.

The sheer scale of Avebury makes it hard to destroy or diminish, regardless of what the centuries have thrown at it. It can be appreciated today much as it would have been four and a half thousand years ago. The concentric circles and rows of stones stretch right across the village, and you can still approach them down roughly the same processional route as its Bronze Age builders. You can even do some of it in a car if you like, using the main Devizes to Swindon road which just ploughs right into the middle of the main circle. Entering this way allows you to share in the drama of its design, the monument opening up before you as you approach. Pass between the marker stones and, bingo, you're part of the ceremonial procession. You might be in a people carrier, but in your mind you've got a blazing torch and deerskin flip-flops.

The integration of the 500-year-old village into the circle maintains the connection between the villagers and their ancient monument. The circle was built by the people of Wiltshire, and their descendants still live in its shadow. It's this matter-of-factness that makes the place so powerful. This circle remains part of the daily life of Avebury, which is as it should be.

No-one will tell you not to touch, or to walk round this way or that. The place is just too big to police in the way Stonehenge is. You can sit on a dolmen and have a pork pie. There's no aura of fuss or fragility about the monument. It's as solid as the Earth. It's enormously reassuring to have a flask of tea or a cigarette leaning against something so powerfully old and manmade. Doing everyday stuff in the presence of an extraordinary ancient landmark is undeniably good for the soul.

The phlegmatic attitude of the Avebury circle has naturally invited a certain blasé lack of respect towards it. It gives the impression that it belongs to the locals so strongly that they've tended to do whatever they fancied with it. By the 1920s, when serious study of the site began, there were plenty of obvious gaps in the rows and circles. Of the 247 stones which experts estimate originally made up Avebury, many had been broken up for use in walls and buildings, some had been buried to clear fields, others had simply fallen over and been carted away. A fair number may even have been toppled deliberately by Christians offended that someone had left a load of pagan symbols on their doorstep.

Alexander Keiller, heir to the Dundee marmalade and butterscotch fortune, excavated and restored many of these missing megaliths in the 1930s as part of his obsession with Avebury, but his work was disturbed by the outbreak of World War II. As recently as 2003, the National Trust discovered even more examples buried beneath the Avebury soil, but say they have no plans to raise them, except as 'computer simulations,' which is frankly cheating. It hardly matters, because the circle retains the power to impress even with sections missing. Because of its sheer size, the loss of a few stones, which would ruin the architecture of a smaller site, has had little effect on the monument's shape. Avebury still looks like what it is – a vast and purposeful artificial landscape. This was a serious engineering job. Whatever it was designed for, it was extremely important to whoever built it.

What exactly that purpose was, we will probably never know. A museum bearing Keiller's name is housed in a barn in the village, filled with odds and ends recovered during his excavations, and allowing visitors to make their own deductions from the evidence. It's the only time you'll be asked to part with any money, and is worth it if you want to find out more about the history of research into the mysterious circles. But the best way to appreciate them is just to stand near them – nearer than you'll be allowed to at any comparably important monument in the country – and wonder at them.

Avebury is one hell of a statement, a massive graffiti tag sprayed over Wiltshire as if to say 'WE WERE HERE'. Ancient people who probably felt vulnerable and lost in the face of the whim of nature, the weather, the passing seasons, gathered together to make their mark. For once, Britons were moulding their environment in a permanent way, a way normally reserved for floodwater, glaciers and wind. Just as they might have done when they constructed the massive artificial hill at Silbury nearby, the builders of Avebury probably stood back, looked at their handiwork and said, 'Ha! We're talking to Mother Nature in a language she can understand. Now let's have a serious chat about all our crops dying last year . . .'

The Avebury monument, from the day it was built, has been about human beings interacting with the landscape. Because you can touch it, lean against it, buy a house in the middle of it, spend some time properly getting to know the thing, it's retained that quality. So, if you're going to visit a stone circle, for goodness' sake go to the one that invites you to share in the history of man's relationship with the very stones of the British Isles. The one down the road might be more famous, but by the way it's behaving at the moment, it thinks you're a cretin.

Christ's House

*Had the creator of Heaven and Earth and E. R. Dexter
and all the goodnesses thereof chosen to address him
in that icy wilderness on the North Wales coast?
Scarcely daring to breathe, he turned. He saw an
impressive figure with a leonine mane of snow-white
hair and an imperious jut to the jaw. Yes, it was God.
And he was wearing MCC suspenders.*

Peter Tinniswood, *Tales From A Long Room*

Welcome to the Garden of Eden. Bedford, birthplace of Ronnie Barker and many a great British van, home of sporting greats Harold

Abrahams, Paula Radcliffe and Eddie 'The Eagle' Edwards, the place where Glenn Miller's band was based and where Bunyan was imprisoned, the place with a ghastly concrete town hall and a one-way system set by Mensa – a middling town in the middle of middle England.

18 Albany Road might as well be 18 Ordinary Road. It's about as predictable an end of terrace house as you'd find anywhere. It's not a tourist attraction and is by no stretch of the imagination a day out. And you can't go in. But, if you're in the area, it's worth driving past, just in case you catch a glimpse of Jesus Christ Himself.

The Ark, as the house is called, has been reserved by an apocalyptic religious sect in preparation for Christ's second coming. When the Lamb of God returns in all His glory, they will give Him the keys, and He'll move in. It's a nice area. All the houses in the street have bucolic names – Penn Dale, Glen Ochil, Ouse View. There are allotments opposite, for Holy pottering around in, and a second-hand car business at the end of the road should He need a runabout for His ministry. He'd be within walking distance of Nando's. At the other end of Albany Road is the very pretty river Ouse, ideal for the occasional stroll along the surface. Christ would like it here.

The story goes something like this. Mabel Barltrop, the widow of a vicar, was released from a lunatic asylum in the 1920s. Changing her name to Octavia, she set up the Panacea Society – a group claiming to be able to cure all the world's ills with the help of the predictions of an early nineteenth-century prophetess called Joanna Southcott, from whose womb Barltrop was now insisting she had been born as the reincarnation of Shiloh, the Messiah.

If it's difficult to believe that Barltrop was the daughter of a woman who had passed away on Xmas Day 1814, more than a hundred years earlier, it's even harder to accept Southcott's claim that she was pregnant with the Messiah two years before her death at the age of 65. The postmortem showed she died a virgin (which is at least in keeping with Christ's previous modus operandi) suffering from dropsy, an accumulation of fluids in the body's cavities. Maybe it was an excess of Holy Spirit.

From the age of eighteen, Southcott had been guided by the 'Spirit of Truth,' as she put it. When she was 42, she was visited by the Lord, who warned of the fate of the earth. She appointed herself God's secretary for the rest of her life, diligently making a note of all His statements regarding the future of mankind, having them witnessed and sealed in packets in The Great Box.

Barltrop established her Panacea Society in Bedford – convinced, as seems patently obvious to just about everybody, that it was the site of the Garden of Eden. She then surrounded herself with twelve 'disciples' who surrendered their worldly goods to her. With the money, she went on a huge property-buying spree, snapping up houses in the town and building a twenty-four-bedroom mansion, The Haven, on the corner of Castle Road and Newnham Road. This will be Earth's control centre when the Messiah shows up.

The twenty-four bedrooms are intended for the twenty-four Church of England bishops Joanna Southcott insisted be present at the opening of her Box, a ceremony which will take place on the day of her 'Great Trial' (still to come), when we will all finally find out what was vouchsafed to her by the Lord over two decades. She'd been trying to assemble her impossible wish-list of bishops for some time, and they had all refused her invitations, sometimes quite rudely. The best she managed was getting three vicars into a room at the same time in 1801.

By the time of her death, Southcott had as many as 100,000 (mainly female) followers and had been ostracised by the (all-male) Church. Membership has declined drastically since then, and today the few remaining devotees are notoriously secretive, claiming to hold Southcott's precious box at an undisclosed location. Solid facts about the sect are difficult to verify, but they're in the phone book, and their assets are believed to total £30m. Their property portfolio runs to twenty-five houses in Bedford, including The Ark.

According to the Society, Christ's house is let on a short lease. The tenants aren't explicitly told whose gaff they're borrowing, and one wonders what their legal position would be in the event of His momentous comeback. Though it's doubtless convenient for the current occupants, the custodians thought long and hard before installing a shower, since they assume that the Messiah will be glowing with love when He shows up and will not need to wash.

The Panacea Society is a breakaway faction from the mainstream of Southcottians, and its private nature does little to discourage rumour. At one point, it was said that the late Diana, Princess of Wales was considered the only person pure enough to bear Shiloh's spirit, which she had done in the shape of Prince William. But this rather voguish thinking seems to have passed out of favour. As does the story that the Second Coming was due while this book was in preparation.

Whatever is in Joanna Southcott's Box is also open to endless speculation, and that's if there's anything left in it anyway. According to some sources, the Box is not in the Society's possession at all, but was given to the British Library in 1966, who examined and filed the contents. The Library have apparently stashed the Box itself in a basement, like something out of *Raiders of the Lost Ark*. Other stories claim the Box has been long mislaid. Whatever the truth, we might not be missing much. Southcott's published writings aren't particularly memorable, apart from the one about the dream in which the bulldog swallows the cat. That's a good one.

But if she was right, and if barmy Mabel Barltrop was right, when Christ returns, he may well take up lodgings here in the Garden of Eden, on the A6 between Luton and Wellingborough. Imagine the thrill of strolling through Bedford one day and bumping into a radiant, unshowered Jesus wandering up Albany Road with a bag of chicken wings. You could dine out on the story for the rest of your life. The wags who never tire of telling you about the time they saw Stephen Fry buying bath olivers at Fortnum's or helped Barbara Windsor jump-start her Jag will find their anecdotes weighed in the balance and found seriously wanting.

We're not guaranteeing it will happen, but if you're passing through Bedford, why not go and have a look? God moves in a mysterious way, and Christ could turn up at any point. If the Panacea Society turns out to have been barking up the right tree all this time, 18 Albany Road could soon be the most famous address in the entire world. Say you saw it first. And don't knock.

Acknowledgements

He is the very pineapple of politeness!
Richard Brinsley Sheridan, *The Rivals*

Thanks are due, firstly, to the many people who own, run and staff the entries in this book. We hope some of their enthusiasm and humour is reflected herein.

Three cheers for Rowland White, with whom the book was conceived, our agent, Cat Ledger, who deserves every penny (plus VAT), and our guardian angels at Penguin, Georgina Atsiaris and the much-missed Abbie Sampson. For their swan-like grace above water whilst paddling frenziedly below the surface, we are indebted to Kate Brunt, Alex Clarke, Helen Eka, John Hamilton, Claire Phillips, Debra Scacco, Ruth Spencer and Rob Williams. Honourable mention is also due to Jon Stock and his staff at the *Daily Telegraph*, who so elegantly serialised the book throughout the summer of 2005.

Our gratitude is also extended to the legion of poor sods who endured our travellers' tales, and laughed at the right (and wrong) bits; the book's first two readers, John Morris and Rebecca Lee, whose observations and clarifications immeasurably improved the manuscript; and the many enthusiasts, friends and like-minded nutters who suggested days out and helped us along the way, including Simon Blackwell, David Bridson, Graham Dury, David Taylor Gooby, Jo Green, Marc Haynes, Mike Hendy, Richard Hurst, Sue Knowles, Andrew Male, Nathalie Manners, Polly Paulusma, John Payne, Sean Powley, Lisa Randall, Lynne Sharp, Dave Standen, Duncan Taylor, Simon Thorpe, Gareth Wall and Guy Walters.

And introducing Stanley Morris, whose conception, construction and arrival in the big silly world coincided with this book's.

By the way, none of us has ever been to Alton Towers. But that's the point.

THE END

Bibliography

AA Illustrated Guide to Britain, Drive Publications
  Ltd, 1971

Ash, Russell, *The Top 10 Of Everything,* Dorling
  Kindersley, 2004

Boyd, Diana, *Brightling Church Guide,* 1979

Brownlee, Nick, *Everything You Didn't Need To Know
  About The UK,* Sanctuary, 2003

Cadbury, Deborah, *The Dinosaur Hunters,* 4th Estate,
  2000

Central Office of Information, *Protect And Survive,*
  HMSO, 1976

Chapman, Graham, *et al., A Liar's Autobiography
  Vol VI,* Methuen, 1980

Clayton, Robert, *Portrait of London,* Hale, 1980

Cope, Julian, *The Modern Antiquarian,* Thorsons,
  1998

Cousins, Julia, *Pitt Rivers Museum,* Pitt Rivers, 1993

'Discovery of Buried Megaliths Completes Avebury
  Circle,' *Independent,* 3 December 2003

Dunn, Tim *Bekonscot Model Village*, Jarrold Publishing

Edelman, Ian, *Discovering Avebury*, Shire Publications, 1985

Ferguson, Euan, 'Alas, people now can't tell their orreries from their elbows,' *Observer*, 16 January 2005

Ferry, Georgina, *A Computer Called LEO*, Fourth Estate, 2003

Fisher, Mark, *Britain's Best Museums And Galleries*, Penguin, 2004

'Ghosts Laid To Rest in The Vaults,' *Scotsman*, 21 May 2003

Headley, Gwyn and Meulenkamp, Wim, *Follies, Grottoes and Garden Buildings*, Aurum Press 1999

Hodges, Andrew, *Alan Turing: The Enigma*, Vintage, 1992

Hunkin, Tim, *Almost Everything There Is To Know*, Hamlyn, 1990

Hutchison, Geoff, *Fuller: The Life And Times Of John Fuller Of Brightling, 1757–1834*, Geoff Hutchison, 1988

Lambton, Lucinda, *A-Z Of Britain*, Harper Collins, 1996

Lawrence, David, *Always A Welcome: The Glove Com-*

partment *History of the Motorway Service Area,* Between Books, 1999

Le Vay, Benedict, *Eccentric Britain,* Bradt, 2000

MacQueen, Adam, *The King Of Sunlight,* Bantam Press, 2004

Musical Instruments Of The World, Paddington, 1976

National Trust, The, *A la Ronde,* The National Trust, 1991

National Trust, The, *Orford Ness,* The National Trust, 1993

Piper, David, *The Companion Guide To London,* Collins, 1964

Sawyer, Rex, *Little Imber On The Down,* Hobnob, 2001

Singh, Simon, *The Code Book,* Fourth Estate, 1999

Society Of Antiquaries Of Newcastle-Upon-Tyne, *Morpeth Chantry Bagpipe Museum Souvenir Guide,* Society Of Antiquaries Of Newcastle-Upon-Tyne, 2003

'You Are Here,' *Guardian,* 16 September 2003

Motor Mania: Concrete Dreams (Flashback for Channel 4, 1996)

One Foot In The Past (BBC2, 1994–1997)

You Either See It Or You Don't (BBC Radio Four, 2001)

Peggy and Sean (www.pegnsean.net)
Public Monument And Sculpture Society, The (www.pmsa.courtauld.ac.uk)
Thrale Family, The (www.thrale.com)
Twentieth Century Society, The (www.c20society. demon.co.uk)
Wikipedia (en.wikipedia.org)

permission of Casarotto Ramsay & Associates. Extract from *Boys From The Black Stuff* by Alan Bleasdale reproduced by permission of The Agency. Extracts from *Under Milk Wood* by Dylan Thomas and *Profiles of the Future* by Arthur C. Clarke reproduced by permission of David Higham Associates. Extract from *In His Own Write* by John Lennon, published by Jonathan Cape. Reprinted by permission of The Random House Group Ltd. Extract from *Seeing Things* by Oliver Postgate reproduced by permission of Sidgwick & Jackson. Extract from *Tales From A Long Room* by Peter Tinniswood reproduced by permission of the estate of the author. Extract from 1940 radio broadcast by Winston Churchill reproduced by permission of Curtis Brown Ltd, London on behalf of the Estate of Sir Winston Churchill.

Every effort has been made to trace copyright holders and we apologise in advance for any unintentional omission. We shall be pleased to add the appropriate acknowledgement to any subsequent edition.

Where they all are

1 Blackgang Chine
2 British Lawnmower Museum
3 Peasholm Park Naval Warfare
4 Louis Tussaud's House of Wax
5 Kelvedon Nuclear Bunker
6 Porteath Bee Centre
7 Mad Jack's Sugar Loaf
8 Keith and Dufftown Railway
9 Eastenders Set
10 Pitt Rivers Museum
11 Eden Ostrich World
12 Keith Harding's World of Mechanical Music
13 Shah Jahan Mosque
14 Beckham Trail
15 Mother Shipton's Cave and Dripping Well
16 Apollo Pavilion
17 Hamilton Toy Collection
18 Imber
19 Cumberland Pencil Museum
20 Pack O'Cards Inn
21 Diggerland
22 Orford Ness
23 Exhibition Road
24 Tebay Services
25 Williamson Tunnels
26 Barometer World
27 Portmeirion
28 Edinburgh Camera Obscura
29 Crystal Palace Dinosaurs
30 House of Marbles
31 Dennis Severs' House
32 Bletchley Park
33 Ripon Tramp Museum
34 Llanfairpwllgwyngyllgogery-chwyrndrobwllllantysiliogogogoch
35 South Bridge Vaults
36 Gnome Magic
37 A La Ronde
38 Port Sunlight
39 Morpeth Bagpipe Museum
40 Bekonscot
41 Avebury Stone Circle
42 Christ's House

Addresses

Blackgang Chine
Near Ventnor
Isle of Wight
PO38 2HN
01983 730052
www.blackgangchine.com

North Bay
Scarborough
North Yorkshire
01723 373333 (Scarborough
Tourist Information
Centre)

The British Lawnmower Museum
106–114 Shakespeare Street
Southport
Lancashire
PR8 5AJ
01704 501336
www.lawnmowerworld.co.uk

Louis Tussaud's House of Wax
18 Regent Road
Great Yarmouth
Norfolk
NR30 2AF
01493 844851

Peasholm Park Naval Warfare
Peasholm Park

Kelvedon Hatch Secret Nuclear Bunker
Kelvedon Hall Lane
Brentwood
Essex

CM14 5TL
01277 364883
www.japar.demon.co.uk

01340 821181
www.keith-dufftown.
org.uk

Porteath Bee Centre
St Minver
Wadebridge
Cornwall
PL27 6RA
01208 863718
www.porteath-
beecentre.co.uk

The EastEnders Set
The environs of BBC
Elstree
Clarendon Road
Borehamwood
Hertfordshire
WD6 1JF

Mad Jack's Sugar Loaf
A field just north of the
B2906 Battle to Heathfield
Road
Nr Wood's Corner
East Sussex

Pitt Rivers Museum
South Parks Road
Oxford
Oxfordshire
OX1 3PP
01865 270927
www.prm.ox.ac.uk

**Keith and Dufftown
Railway**
Dufftown Station
Dufftown
Banffshire
AB55 4BA

Eden Ostrich World
Langwathby Hall Farm
Langwathby
Penrith
Cumbria
CA10 1LW

01768 881771
www.ostrich-world.com

Keith Harding's World of Mechanical Music
The Oak House
High Street
Northleach
Gloucestershire
GL54 3ET
01451 860181
www.mechanicalmusic.
co.uk

Shah Jahan Mosque
149 Oriental Road
Woking
Surrey
GU22 7BA
01483 760679 to arrange a
visit
www.shahjahanmosque.
org.uk

The Beckham Trail
Various locations between
Walthamstow and
Chingford
North East London
020 8496 3000 (Waltham
Forest Council)
www.lbwf.gov.uk/index/
leisure/places-of-interest/
beckham-trail

Mother Shipton's Cave and Dripping Well
Prophesy House
Knaresborough
North Yorkshire
HG5 8DD
01423 864600
www.mothershiptonscave.
com

Apollo Pavilion
Nr Helford Road
Sunny Blunts Housing
Estate
Peterlee
County Durham

Hamilton Toy Collection
111 Main Street
Callander
Perthshire
FK17 8BQ
01877 330004

Imber
Near Heytesbury
Salisbury Plain
Wiltshire
01980 620819 (Salisbury
Plain Army Training
Estate)
www.public-interest.co.uk/
imber
(Open during most of
August)

**The Cumberland Pencil
Museum**
Southey Works
Greta Bridge
Keswick
Cumbria
CA12 5NG

01768 773626
www.pencils.co.uk*

Pack O'Cards Inn
High Street
Combe Martin
Devon
EX34 OET
01271 882300
www.packocards.co.uk

Diggerland
Medway Valley Leisure
Park
Roman Way
Strood
Kent
ME2 2NU
08700 344437
www.diggerland.com
(Other sites at Langley
Park, County Durham and
Verbeer Manor,
Cullompton, Devon)

*That's a proper web
address, isn't it?

Orford Ness
The National Trust Quay
Office
Orford Quay
Orford
Woodbridge
Suffolk
IP12 2NU
01394 450900
www.nationaltrust.org.uk/
orfordness

**The Wellcome Collection
of Medical History**
(within The National
Museum of Science and
Industry)
Exhibition Road
South Kensington
London
SW7 2DD
0870 870 4868
www.sciencemuseum.
org

The Cast Courts (within
the Victoria and Albert
Museum)
Cromwell Road
South Kensington
London
SW7 2RL
020 7942 2000
www.vam.ac.uk

Tebay Services
The M6 (just north of
Junction 38)
Old Tebay
Penrith
Cumbria
CA10 3SS
01539 624505
www.westmorland.com

**Williamson Tunnels
Heritage Centre**
The Old Stableyard
Smithdown Lane
Liverpool
Merseyside

L7 3EE
0151 709 6868
www.williamsontunnels.
co.uk

Barometer World
Quicksilver Barn
Merton
Devon
EX20 3DS
01805 603443
www.barometerworld.co.uk

Portmeirion
Gwynedd
LL48 6ET
01766 770000
www.portmeirion-village.
com

**Camera Obscura and
World of Illusions**
Castlehill
The Royal Mile
Edinburgh
EH1 2ND

0131 226 3709
www.camera-obscura.co.uk

**The Dinosaur Park and
Tidal Lake**
Crystal Palace Park
Thicket Road
Penge
London
SE20 8DT
020 8778 9496 (Park
Ranger's Office)
www.bromley.gov.uk/
leisure/
parksandcountryside/
crystal-palace-park.htm

House of Marbles
The Old Pottery
Pottery Road
Bovey Tracey
Devon
TQ13 9DS
01626 835358
www.houseofmarbles.com

Dennis Severs' House
18 Folgate Street
Spitalfields
London
E1 6BX
020 7247 4013
www.dennissevershouse.
co.uk

Bletchley Park
Wilton Avenue
Bletchley
Milton Keynes
Bedfordshire
MK3 6EB
01908 640404
www.bletchleypark.org.uk

The Workhouse Museum
Allhallowgate
Ripon
North Yorkshire
HG4 1LE
01765 690799
www.riponmuseums.co.uk

**Llanfairpwllgwyngyllgo-
gerychwyrndrobwllllan-
tysiliogogogoch**
Isle of Anglesey
www.llanfairpwllgwyn-
gyllgogerychwyrndro-
bwllllantysilio
gogogoch.co.uk

The Vaults Tour
South Bridge
Edinburgh
0131 557 6464
www.mercattours.com
(Tour departs from
Mercat Cross, High Street,
Royal Mile)

Gnome Magic
Old Ipswich Road
Dedham
Colchester
Essex
CO7 6HU
01206 231390
www.gnomemagic.co.uk

A la Ronde
Summer Lane
Exmouth
Devon
EX8 5BD
01395 265514
www.nationaltrust.org.uk

Port Sunlight
Wirral
Merseyside
0151 644 6466 (Port
Sunlight Heritage Centre)
www.portsunlightvillage.
com

**Morpeth Bagpipe
Museum**
The Chantry
Bridge Street
Morpeth
Northumberland
NE61 1PD
01670 500717
www.bagpipemuseum.org.uk

Bekonscot Model Village
Warwick Road
Beaconsfield
Buckinghamshire
HP9 2PL
01494 672919
www.bekonscot.co.uk

Avebury
Nr Marlborough
Wiltshire
SN8 1RF
01672 539250
www.nationaltrust.org.uk

Christ's House
18 Albany Road
Bedford
Bedfordshire
(Not open to the public)

An Uncommonly British Index